STRIPPING PINE

'Her advice is of the basic, useful kind that comes from a lot of experience.'

Daily Telegraph

'Considerable expertise . . . Pat Cutforth does not hesitate to state the seemingly obvious so, even if you have no skills, you will be able to follow her instructions.'

Ideal Home

'Instructions are sensible and written in a matter-of-fact style . . . essential reading before you pull on the rubber gloves.'

Home Improvements Guide

STRIPPING PINE

and other woods

PAT CUTFORTH

JOHN MURRAY

First published 1983
by John Murray (Publishers) Ltd
50 Albemarle Street, London W1X 4BD
Reprinted 1984

Typeset by Inforum Ltd, Portsmouth
Printed and bound in Great Britain
by The Pitman Press, Bath

British Library Cataloguing in Publication Data
Cutforth, Pat
Stripping pine and other woods.
1. Furniture finishing—Amateurs' manuals
I. Title
684.1'0443 TT199.4
ISBN 0–7195–4069–0

To ***Mary***

who made me write it

Contents

Introduction

In the last ten years pine furniture has gained tremendously in popularity, so that old and attractive pieces command very high prices. It has even achieved the distinction of being faked. In the midst of this enthusiasm, perhaps we should remember that most of this furniture was intended to be functional. Carpenters who could not afford the cabinet woods for basic items of furniture, made them of cheap pine, and often painted them – the same disguise that we now use for plywood and whitewood.

Pine furniture came at the bottom of the scale which started with beautiful craftsman-made furniture of walnut and mahogany. Then followed the humbler country copies of these fine pieces, this time in oak, elm, beech and other home-grown woods. Lastly came our painted pine furniture, still copying the fashionable styles. With each drop down the quality scale, there was a corresponding time lag in style, so that a 'Georgian' chest of drawers in pine may well have been made much later than its mahogany counterpart. It took a while for fashion to filter down to the country carpenter, and he would go on using a successful style long after the London craftsmen had moved on to something else. A perfect example of this is the Windsor chair in its various forms, still being made and bought after 200 years. But pine is not just a copying wood. Because it is soft and easy to work, carpenters were often inspired to create fanciful designs never found in hardwood furniture. Some pieces of furniture are ornamented with carving, turning or fretwork, others are a curious but appealing amalgam, like the chest of drawers cum washstand in figure 1.

The quality of this pine furniture varied greatly: some was very skillfully built, some crudely nailed together. Because the construction details would be hidden under the paint, the carpenter could give less care to the finish. Thus, a stripped piece of furniture may have the dowels or pegs showing at every joint, instead of their being inserted from the back. Little blobs of white filler appear, covering nailheads, or filling in the irregularities of

Fig 1

knots. Luckily, none of these marks on the surface is considered to detract from the desirability of a piece, and indeed, like knots, they are often thought to enhance it.

What has caused this upsurge in the popularity of pine furniture? All woods have the virtue of variety of surface texture and colour. In addition, pine is pale, and particularly soft and attractive when used in decorating, as anyone who has replaced a mahogany chest of drawers with a pine one will know. The light wood cheers up a room, much as painting the woodwork white instead of brown would do. Pine blends well with paint or wallpaper of any colour, and the varied surface texture makes the wood seem to recede. I noticed this myself in a narrow back hall which was lined down one side with painted cupboards. When I stripped them, the room immediately seemed wider, while the cupboards themselves became a visual asset. I believe that it is because one can 'look into' the wood, rather than being bounced away by the flat paint surface. This quality of seeming to recede makes large and ungainly pieces of furniture appear smaller and more appealing.

Another point to remember is that pine furniture is still *comparatively* cheap. Compared, that is, with a corresponding piece in a hardwood like mahogany. If you are attempting to furnish a house with some bits of period furniture, then pine is certainly a better bet. If you live in a period house, or even one built before 1940 or so, you have a good chance of finding built-in furniture which will look lovely when stripped: the doors to the airing cupboard, perhaps, or a corner cupboard in the bathroom. However plain it looks when painted, it will be a definite asset when stripped. Doors can be removed to your caustic soda bath, the frames dealt with *in situ* with a proprietary paint stripper.

A major virtue of pine furniture is that it lives happily in any room in the house. Small pieces look just right in a child's bedroom, and big cupboards and dressers blend with the most modern kitchen. Even in a tiny bathroom a set of shelves or a little cupboard may provide the finishing decorative touch. Depending on its style and quality, pine furniture can look equally at home in a boot hall or a formal drawing room.

One final point is that natural wood requires no maintenance beyond the occasional polish – no more repainting of doors.

And now, where can you find these pieces waiting to be stripped?

2 · Where to look

Auctions

Buying a piece of furniture at an auction is very exciting. The atmosphere is charged with competition and optimism, and the way the bidding goes is unpredictable. Sometimes you are braced for a battle over a piece of furniture that seems utterly desirable, and then no one is interested. At other times, all the prices are high and you might as well give up and go home. There are disappointments, like discovering that several of a set of chairs are riddled with woodworm, and this is why you *must* go to auction previews, or arrive early enough on the day to take a look before the sale begins. My worst folly is deciding I want something as it is held up for auction, when I have not previously looked it over. 'Job lots' are particularly tempting. This is the way to collect non-working vacuum cleaners, broken china and superfluous firescreens.

At the viewing you will inevitably discover that the lots you want are numbered 109 and 385. Auctioneers generally get through about 100 lots an hour, so you have the option of going home in the middle if you live nearby. Alternatively, you can arrive with a sandwich and a book and settle in for the day. You can also leave bids with the auctioneer, though I prefer to bid in person because you can 'feel' how it is going. Too often a bid which has been left is used as the starting figure by the auctioneer, and while it may go no higher, it is galling to think you have paid more than you need.

It is certainly important to have a top price fixed in your mind, even if you are there. The best way is to decide what it is worth *to you*, though there are many price guides on the market if you are really at sea. One such is *Miller's Price Guide to Pine Furniture and Kitchenalia.* I usually fix on an uneven sum like £10.50, in the hope that others will stop when they reach the round figure. If you drop out of the bidding and minutes later regret it, you can speak to the buyer afterwards and see if he will sell it to you. He may want it very much himself, but possibly be tempted by a quick profit. In the case of job lots, he may not even want the item you were bidding for. I once acquired a huge unwanted box of Kilner fruit bottling jars when bidding for a small glass lampshade. Afterwards I heard two women discussing how sad they were at missing these same jars, but I did not quite have the courage to approach them. There is a happy ending to this story, because several years later, some friends of my sister came to visit from the United States. Their last name was Kilner, and their grandfather had invented The Jar. They were thrilled when I showed them my box of antique, rusty-topped glass jars, and reverently carried some home.

The auctions I have been describing are monthly or fortnightly country sales. Buy a local paper and look for the advertisements of sales. If they describe a coming auction as limited to, say, only pictures or silver, then it is probably too high-powered. On the other hand, an 'Important Sale of Antique and Other Furniture and Effects' may be a fairly junky monthly sale in the town hall. Go to a couple of viewings. You will soon recognise the calibre of the sale from the items on view. Talk to auction-going friends and ask their advice. Even at a rather grand auction, there is always the chance of a bargain, because although dealers will be present, they have to think of a mark-up on the price they pay. On the other hand, the person you are bidding against may not be a dealer at all, but another keen householder prepared to go to any price.

Some pieces of furniture are of no interest to dealers. They may have plywood panels, which disqualifies them as antiques, or be the type of furniture which is not readily saleable, such as a very large wardrobe. Or there may be too many repairs needed to an otherwise attractive piece. For the auction-goer, all this is good news. The plywood panels can be disguised, and the cupboard may be exactly the right size for an awkward situation. The wardrobe can be taken apart and used for various other projects. Do not expect great bargains in chests of drawers, desks or dressers. These are all eminently saleable and much sought after. My best finds have either been well disguised, or only desirable to me. One such is a small mahogany table with a drawer, which was covered in paint. It had two-inch stumps sticking up at all four corners, showing it to have been a narrow washstand with a top shelf, of the kind now commonly used as bedside tables. I stripped it, chiselled the stumps down to match the moulding round the edge, and sealed and polished it. It is now a beautiful small occasional table (figure 2).

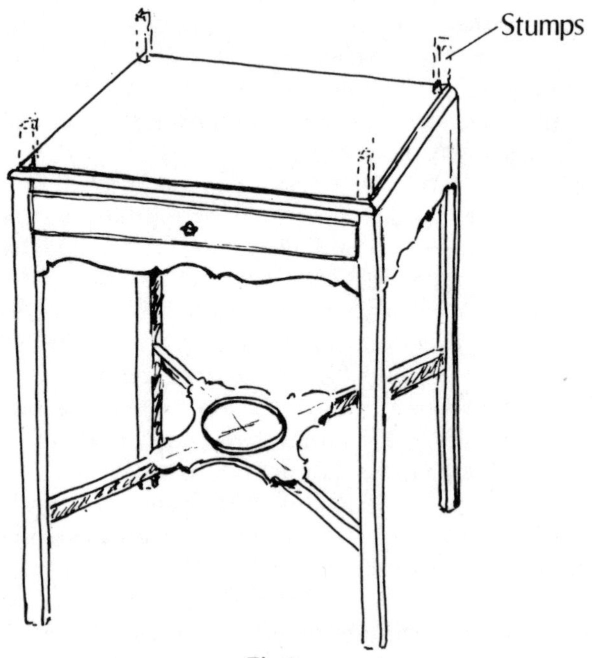

Fig 2

If you get hooked on auctions, you will get to know the dealers and other buyers. They are usually friendly and helpful, will advise you on prices generally, and have been known to say, 'If you want that, I won't bid for it'. I suppose this can become a mild form of Dealer's Ring, in that it can keep the price down, but I have not noticed anything really sinister in that line. Imaginary bids are sometimes taken against a reserve or an over-keen bidder, so I sometimes allow a little hesitation to appear in my bidding. Of course this may have the reverse effect, encouraging a real opponent to think he is winning!

There is one very entertaining form of auction, and that is the

House Sale. This is in fact a sale of the house contents – or that part of them that remains when the Chippendale chairs have been removed to Sothebys. Here you have a chance to buy furnishings as well as furniture, and you can walk around the house looking at everything in its place. The quality of the furnishing will probably be better than you can normally afford, because you will find things for sale which were very expensive when new, and are now a bargain.

At the grander type of house sale they may erect a marquee on the day, and the sense of occasion sometimes attracts local residents who can push the bidding up dramatically. Good bargains can still be had, especially at the rather humbler sale, where the auctioneer moves through the house, taking the bids as he goes. At either sort, you will be expected to remove any lots that you have bought on that same day, so be prepared. Keep your usual vigilance about the state of the furniture you want to buy. Some friends once bid on impulse for an Edwardian china cabinet which was tied to a tent pole in a marquee, never wondering why, till they went to collect it and it fell over. It is worth mentioning that they paid £10 for it, and sold it for £170 ten years later.

Jumble sales

Jumble sales give the same sense of anticipation as auctions: there is always the chance of a Find. The key to success here is to arrive early, and be there when the doors open. Prices will depend on the knowledge of the person running the sale. One seldom finds large pieces of furniture at a jumble sale, but boxes, mirrors and other small items do turn up amongst the bric à brac. As with auctions, you have to attend a lot of jumble sales to find something particular, and often there is nothing but rubbish. One tip: If you are debating about buying something, pick it up, or someone else will.

Stripped pine shops

Even the keenest stripper can find that there are one or two pieces of furniture that just don't turn up locally. In despair you can turn to one of the many shops dealing in pine furniture.

Many antique shops have occasional pieces of pine, but for a wider selection, seek out a specialist shop. Prices vary considerably from area to area, so it is a good idea to shop around. If you are looking for something specific ask the proprietor to show you what he has in that line. Often there is stock due into the shop, or standing outside partially stripped, and something there might be just right. If there is a piece that has been stripped but not sanded or polished, you may be able to buy it at a reduced price and do the finishing yourself.

Buying furniture from a dealer is expensive compared with stripping something yourself, but you pay for his time and expertise, and occasionally it's worth it. For instance, I recently bought a pine bed from a dealer, because I have never managed to find one at an auction. If you cannot immediately see what you want in a shop, the dealer may be able to find it for you, given time. Take any appropriate measurements with you – length of wall for a dresser, for instance – and check ceiling heights, because dressers and wardrobes are often very tall, though they may not appear so in the shop.

If you are buying a table, ask about the finish. It will probably be wax, which is not at all practical (see page 45), and it is as well to be warned. If polyurethane, do not be deterred by the glassy finish. Varnish is an ideal surface for functional pieces, and is very attractive when rubbed down and waxed. Be sure to look furniture over carefully before you buy it, and check any working parts. Pull drawers in and out, sit on chairs, lift up table flaps. You will often find that handles, plinths, mouldings or other details have been added, and a close inspection will reveal differences in the colour of the wood, holes from old fitments or other signs of change. Whether you object depends on how much you mind, and the price being asked for the furniture.

One other warning about shops: you may be delighted by the supply of small cupboards, sets of shelves and framed mirrors, but after a while you will notice that there are duplicates. There is such a demand for these small items that many dealers have a carpenter who makes them for him out of old wood. Unless mirror glass is bevelled and obviously fits its frame, this is probably an old picture frame stripped of veneer. The dealer will tell you which things are newly made, *if* you ask.

Sale advertisements

Local papers carry advertisements of items for sale. 'Old painted chest of drawers' is an obviously hopeful one, while 'dropleaf table and matching chairs' is less so. A phone call will clarify matters. It is important to get the paper the moment it comes out, because anything good goes quickly. Sometimes shops have noticeboards with local ads pinned up, but these generally feature a lot of old bicycles and prams.

Dumps

Anything can turn up on the municipal dump; it is merely a question of having the nerve to go and look. Out-dated furniture is still thrown out by the unknowing, especially kitchen cupboards and tables. Outside an auction room before a sale, you may find similar dumped objects which you can have for nothing, but ask.

Demolition sites

I have to confess that I have never tried this source, but only from cowardice. I know that old doors and other fittings can often be purchased from the foreman on a site. There is now a large business in buying up architectural components from buildings that are being demolished. There are likewise shops selling these same components back to the general public. If you want pillars, a fireplace, a staircase or a gazebo, you could seek out one of these shops. These entrepreneurs are not likely to be interested in an ordinary derelict old house in the country, so if you see one being pulled down, apply directly to the foreman, who may ask only a nominal sum. And of course, anything thrown onto a builder's skip is fair game.

Around your own house

In most houses built before 1940 there are some built-in pieces of furniture which might profitably be stripped: a corner cupboard, perhaps, or an old press in the kitchen. Sometimes there is a wooden paint cupboard in the garage which, looked at more closely, proves to have nice panelled doors. They can be unscrewed and removed outdoors for easy stripping. The indoor work is more daunting, and I am ashamed to admit that I have one or two fine wood doors with painted architraves round them.

Relations and friends may have pieces of furniture that they do not value and might let you experiment on. I have just looked out of a window and seen that my friends are using an old solid oak tilt-top table as a garden table. It looks grey and bedraggled in the rain, and would require some work to make it beautiful again – but well worth it.

Keep your eyes open wherever you are, whether poking through Grandmother's attic or passing a junk shop in a strange town. With experience, your ability to spot things will grow, though it is easier if you already have the jumble sale mentality. When you have once stripped an unprepossessing piece of furniture and seen the transformation that can be effected, you will be hooked on stripping.

2 · What to look for

When wandering round a saleroom or looking over old furniture, there are certain useful bits of information to bear in mind. Elimination tips can save a lot of wasted time and money. I have divided these pointers into two groups, the first dealing with general aspects of looking at and choosing furniture, the second taking individual types one at a time. The first and most important of the general pointers is:

How to recognise woods

This is not an easy thing to establish. It is a help to learn to recognise some common woods in their polished state, especially pine, beech, elm and oak. I have developed some little hints on recognition for myself, and I will pass them on to you, but the best thing of all is to look at actual pieces of wood. I will start with the hardwoods – oak, elm and beech. The term 'hardwood' means the timber from broad-leaved deciduous trees, and is not a reference to the strength or resilience of the wood.

Oak and **Elm** are both fairly dark in colour and have a coarse, open grain. If you run your nail across it, it feels bumpy and ridged. The grain in both is mainly straight, though wavy growth rings can be seen on large surfaces. The main differences between the two are as follows: oak, if it is cut a certain way, has a characteristic 'silver-grain' figure, which looks like silvery eels swimming across the grain, and once seen is unmistakeable. The grain itself appears to be made up of long scratched lines, whereas in elm, the grain looks more like a series of small dots and hatch marks.

Beech has a very fine straight grain, so the surface feels quite smooth to the touch. This fine grain distinguishes it easily from oak or elm, but not so easily from pine, except that it is virtually free of knots. The wood is flecked with small brown dashes along the grain, and like oak, it has a 'silver-grain' pattern. In the case of beech, the streaks are much smaller, so they look like tadpoles swimming over the grain. It is now very obvious to me whether I am looking at beech or pine, but this 'tadpole test' used to be my main way of telling them apart. Beech is stronger and lighter than pine, and can be used in thinner sections without breaking. Spindly or bowed legs and fine turnings usually point to beech.

Pine is a word that covers many members of the conifer family (the softwoods), from Scots Fir to Redwood. The pine we normally meet is a yellow wood, which darkens to a warm honey-brown with age and exposure to air. Knots are dotted through it, and the grain swirls round them in a most attractive way. (If they do not seem to be part of the pattern but are separate and black-ringed, they are dead knots, which tend to fall out.) The grain itself looks as if someone has dipped a fine brush in some sepia paint and drawn long lines down the wood, sometimes many close together, sometimes fatter ones more widely spaced. The surface of the wood is smooth to touch.

Pitch-Pine (also called Western Pine) is a resinous wood which is darker and redder than normal pine. The grain is fairly similar, except that there is more variety of colour and density, which can give it a striped look. Some of the grain lines stand up in ridges, especially in table tops, where the softer parts of the wood have worn down. A final pointer is that it is immensely heavy. It was extensively used for school desks, flooring and church furniture, and most old pews and settles are of pitch-pine.

Deal is another word for pine, and is actually a timber term meaning a small plank. It has a rather derogatory ring to it: 'It's only an old bit of deal'.

Before setting out to your first auction, it is a good idea to look around your house to familiarise yourself with the various woods. If you have an old kitchen chair, the seat is probably elm and the legs and back beech. If you can also line up a piece of oak for comparison, you will quickly see all the differences I have been describing. Of course you will make mistakes, and meet other woods that I have not included, but these are the ones you are most likely to confuse with pine. Your library will have descriptive books on wood if you want to probe further.

Likely coverings

Your potential piece of pine may be hidden under paint, brown varnish, fake ebony black varnish, or some coats of all of these.

The crucial thing is the very bottom layer. To find out what this is, take a coin or key and flake off a bit of the finish in an unobtrusive place. (In a saleroom you will probably find that a dealer has already done this for you). If you can see clear wood, then all is well, but if a red stain is left, beware! This stain is the penetrating pigment of an old brown paint or stain, and is fairly common. It is difficult to remove, though it can be minimized with a medium brown stain applied on top of the red, after you have stripped the piece (see p. 52). If you desperately want the piece of furniture, it may be worth the effort involved, and you should be able to get it quite cheaply.

If you are uncertain what wood a piece is made of, open a door or drawer and look inside the front, where it is usually not painted. You will be able to see the characteristic grain markings – and knots, if it is pine. Remember that the colour will be subdued because the wood is unfinished on the inside, so to get some idea of its real colour, lick your finger and wet a patch of the wood.

Proportions

No amount of stripping can change the proportions of a piece of furniture. It can certainly reduce its apparent size, but the better the original shape, the more pleased you will be with the final result. On the other hand, if the proportions are good, even the plainest old cupboard can look really pretty. Stand back and take a good look at it, mentally adding feet or a plinth, if they are missing.

Construction and age

These are not desperately important factors if you are simply after something decorative, but they may explain a sudden rush of interested bidding at an auction. Certain points in construction give a rough indication of age. For instance, square-headed nails were not much used after the middle of the nineteenth century, when machines took over their production. Dovetail joints, always a sign of quality, are irregular when made by hand, (figure 3) and there tend to be fewer of them. If you look at the rough planks at the back of standing furniture, like dressers and wardrobes, you may be able to see saw marks. Circular marks

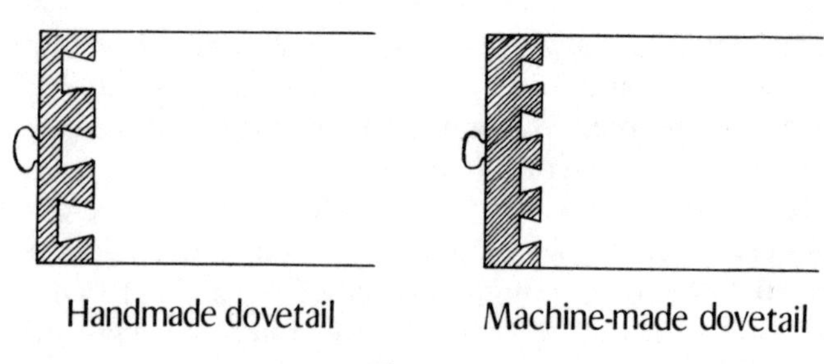

Fig 3

indicate that the wood was cut after 1850, when the circular saw was invented. In general, handmade construction is imperfect. Nails and screws look wavy and rough, dovetails vary in size, and the surface of the wood will have a hand-planed look. None of these details will be immediately obvious, because they are concealed in the frame and under the finish of a piece of furniture – you will have to look for them. Fakery is not usually a problem in *painted* pine furniture, though details like handles and knobs may have been added or taken away over the years. *Stripped* pine is a different matter. If you are buying something already stripped, look it over very carefully for added glazing bars or bits of moulding which might add to the apparent age (and the price) of the piece. Additions are usually visible through a slight difference in colour, a roughness in the finish, or a general look of not belonging.

Brass fittings

Knobs, handles and locks are a good clue to the age of a piece of furniture, if they are the originals. Take a glance at the inside of the drawer front to find out; if they are not original, there will be telltale screw holes, or a round plug from a knob. The shape of a Georgian or Art Nouveau brass escutcheon plate is easy to recognise and so is the uncompromising Victorian knob. Late in the nineteenth century, cheap stamped metal plates were introduced, though the better quality furniture still had solid cast brass. Most handles and plates of this period, and on into the twentieth century, were 'face-fixed', that is held in place by visible brass screws or nails on the front, whereas earlier handles were bolted through the drawers. I have drawn (figures 4 and 5) a

HANDLES

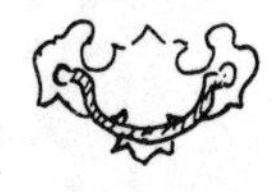
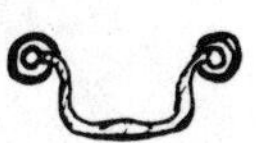

GEORGIAN

LATE GEORGIAN

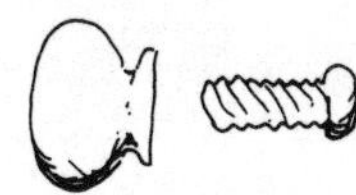
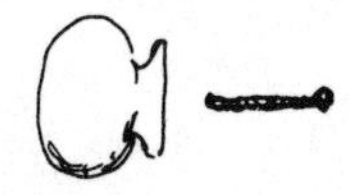

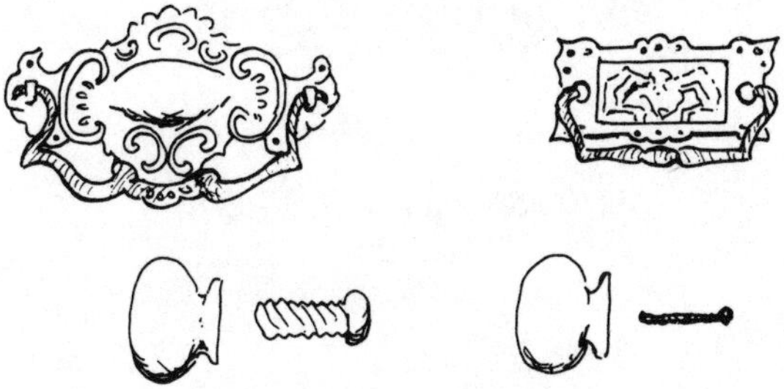

VICTORIAN

TURN OF THE CENTURY

Fig 4

HANDLES

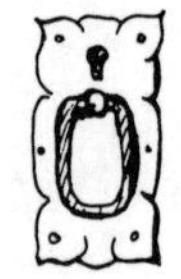

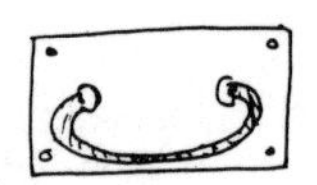

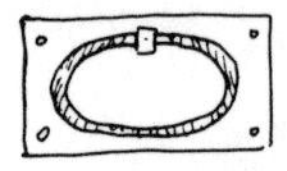

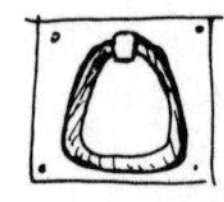

PRESSED METAL PLATES

VICTORIAN REPRODUCTIONS
(on oak)

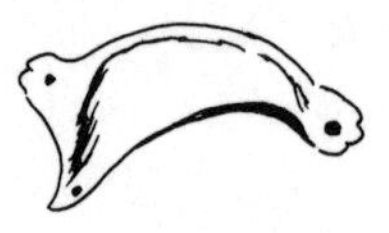

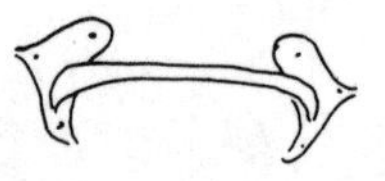

ART NOUVEAU

Fig 5

variety of handles with their approximate dates, because this is one of the most helpful aids in identifying different styles of furniture, and the woods they are probably made of.

Plates and handles are often covered in so many layers of paint or varnish that it is impossible to tell what lies underneath, so carry a small magnet with you – brass fittings will not attract it, base metal will.

Details

The more of these the better. Any mouldings, carving, panels, beading or other details give a piece of furniture individuality. When stripped, they show up surprisingly well, and make a great difference to the general effect of the piece. In a shop, they will add considerably to the price; for this reason, they are sometimes superimposed on a mediocre piece of furniture. As a general guide to the age of a door, it is useful to know that up to the turn of the century most panels had strips of moulding around the edge, where they met the frame. In Edwardian times, panels were set into square-edged frames.

Woodworm

Woodworm is bad news. The holes are not always easy to spot, and even one or two can betoken a vast network inside. It is important to look in the less accessible parts of the furniture: the inside of chair legs and under the frame of the seat, in the backs of cupboards, etc. Woodworm like bare unfinished wood best, and have a preference for cane, elm and beech. In all woods they are particularly attracted to the sapwood – the light-coloured softer wood on the edge of a plank.

New holes look pale and fresh, and often a little sawdust will pour out if the piece is tipped up. A lot of holes means that the section of wood will be weakened, and the attack difficult to deal with effectively. If the infestation is slight, you can treat it with woodworm killing fluid, and I recommend the Rentokil squeezy injector bottle. It shoots the fluid into the holes with such force that it often comes squirting out of another hole some distance away. Check for new holes after a week or so, in case there is a new hatch.

Stability

Unless you are a handyman, avoid the really decrepit pieces. Sagging cupboards, chairs with one leg missing, are best left for others. On the other hand, broken hinges and locks, or missing hardware, can all be replaced very easily. Read Chapter 5 for ideas on easy repairs. Some are mentioned when they apply to individual pieces of furniture, in the section which follows.

FURNITURE TYPES

Dressers

Dressers are always expensive no matter what state they are in, because everyone wants them. Look for the general details of beading, moulding, etc. Make sure that the top matches the bottom before being tempted to pay a high price, because these were often married – that is to say, two separate pieces were put together for convenience, and do not actually make one piece of furniture. These are the points to look for: any locks, knobs, handles or mouldings should match, and the top should fit comfortably onto the bottom.

Ideally the backs of dressers should be open, or made of planks, or of tongue and groove boarding. Plywood is not a good sign, though it may be a replacement. These backs are often surprisingly crude, the boards hardly even planed – like bits of an old crate. A coat of paint on the inside improves them, and will disguise plywood.

When buying a dresser, it is sensible to be realistic about its function. A bottom cupboard is really more useful in a kitchen, for instance, than an open 'pot shelf' or drawers (I know this to my cost).

Chests of drawers

Those with swing mirrors on top are generally not very old. Sometimes they are not even pine, but an unattractive close-grained wood with greyish streaks. This is called 'satin walnut', though it is actually the wood of a South American gum tree, and it was much used in Edwardian times for bedroom furniture. To check on the wood, open a drawer and look inside for the familiar knotty pattern.

You can tell a lot from the feet: if there are none, and the chest of drawers rests directly on the ground, looking squat and out of proportion, it may have had bun feet. These are a bit like very large turned knobs, one on each corner, and they are prone to break off if the chest is moved around roughly. If you tilt it back, the round marks and screw holes left by the feet show up clearly on the bottom. You may be able to get replacements from a dealer, because they are often removed, along with wooden knobs, in favour of Georgian-styled features (see p. 63). If a chest of drawers has not been stripped or altered and has bracket or ogee feet (figure 6), then it is probably 150 or more years old. You would be pretty lucky to find one of these.

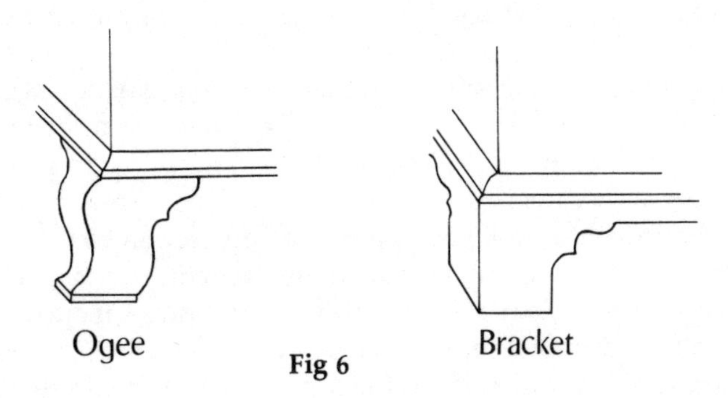

Fig 6

Broken or missing knobs are not a problem. You can usually find some in the reject-pile of the afore-mentioned dealer, or replace them with new knobs or brass handles.

The top of a chest of drawers is important. Bits broken off edges or corners are extremely difficult to mend satisfactorily, likewise great splits along the grain. You may feel you can live with splits, if they do not distort the whole top, or they can be filled, if slight. Stains and burns can be minimised (see Chapter 5).

Check the running of the drawers. If they are merely sticky, you can ease them with some wax, but a lot of movement from side to side means structural problems. Some minor repairs can be handled by the unskilled, and it might be as well to read through the section of Chapter 5 which deals with drawers and runners. This will give you more of an idea of what faults to look for, and whether you will be able to fix them when found.

Tables

Pine tables were mainly meant for use in kitchens, not dining rooms, except in the humbler houses. Decorative dining room tables were made out of the cabinet woods – oak, walnut, mahogany, rosewood. The ones with a support framework underneath – refectory or trestle tables – are generally made of oak, and oak or mahogany was often used for gate-leg and draw-leaf tables. This is not to say that absolutely no formal tables were made of pine, but just to warn the unwary buyer that the demand for them has led to large numbers being made up out of old wood. This is the result of the upgrading of pine furniture from kitchen to dining room status.

Kitchen tables were simply made; four legs, a plain planked top, and perhaps a drawer or two. The top is the most important feature. Ideally it should be quite thick, and free from splits. These occur because the top has been fixed firmly in place, allowing no leeway for expansion and contraction (see Chapter 5). The top can be removed and pulled together with glue and sash cramps, but it is a major project, and one I try to avoid. However, small tables tops, two foot wide or less, can be mended with a tourniquet (page 53). If the top is marked, but fairly thick, it can be planed until an acceptable surface is reached. My own kitchen table was originally covered in formica, and when I ripped this off ('chipped' might be a better word), I had to plane away about an eighth of an inch to remove bits of glue, chips, holes, etc. If you are faced with such a table, you can get a good idea of what you will find under the formica, by crawling under the table and looking at the underside of the top. If woodworm holes are visible, remember that too much planing will expose the rabbit warren of tunnels underneath. In a table top with woodworm holes *and* several layers of paint, just stripping it may reveal the tunnels, because the woodworm are probably using the paint as their roof, rather than a skin of wood.

Tables are quite a hefty project to strip, but one comfort is that they look quite good with the tops stripped and the base left painted or stained. Many kitchen tables were meant to be like this, and the tops were scrubbed daily by housewife or maid. On older tables, you often find square legs – usually quite fat and slightly tapered, like elephantine Hepplewhite. The ones most easily found have turned legs, some of them almost as thick as piano legs. Don't despair – the top is all anyone will really notice.

Apart from the large central kitchen table, numerous side tables were also made. A great variety of these can still be found, and as a general rule, the plainer they are, the cheaper. Drawers, galleries round the top, pretty tapered legs, all mean a potential upgrade to 'writing table', and corresponding rise in price.

Blanket boxes and chests

Blanket boxes are easy to find, though their condition may vary. Make sure that the top is in good condition, or be prepared to cover it. Older boxes were made from very few pieces of wood, sometimes just six planks in all: two sides, front and back, top and bottom. Boxes made out of a hardwood such as elm are very desirable, and can sometimes be found cheaply, but look out for woodworm. If you find an old wooden trunk or chest with a domed lid, and covered in 'leather' paper, beware! I once took the paper off one of these only to find that the wood underneath was unplaned, and as rough as an orange box.

Features which add to the value of these pieces are candle boxes (shallow open boxes fixed to an inside side), and drawers in the base of the chest, when it becomes a 'mule chest'.

Chairs

Stability is the important feature here. On the whole, old chairs were very sturdily made, and many have survived. The most common problem is a wobbly back. It is surprisingly difficult to put this right, because the uprights were generally fixed into the seat with wedges, but I have some wobbly-backed chairs that are still going strong after eight years of constant use. On a scroll-back chair, make sure that the scroll has not broken off. Because the grain of the wood runs up and down the uprights of a chair, there is a weak point just where the scroll curves over (figure 7) and this piece often snaps off.

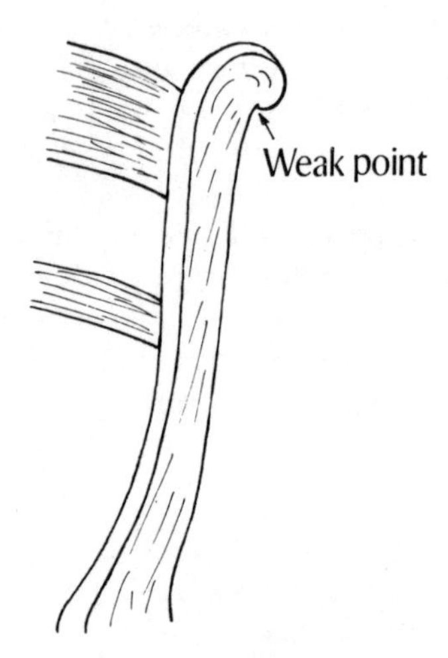

Fig 7

Legs are another possible trouble spot. Loose ones can be mended with glue, and a missing cross-bar can be improvised with a shaped piece of dowel. Look at the bottom of the legs. Have they been cut off? there should be a straight piece, about four inches long, below the bottom turned spindle. Because chair legs sometimes got wet, chewed by dogs, pushed around, etc. they often had to be cut down to find sound wood. Sometimes there is no straight piece left at all, so that the bottom turning rests on the floor. Obviously this makes them too low for normal use (figure 8).

Be sure to check carefully for woodworm. Country chairs made for kitchens and cottages had elm seats and turned beech legs, both of which are particularly relished by woodworm. Turn all chairs over and look under the seat and inside the legs. Don't assume because one or two chairs in a set are free of woodworm, that the others will be.

The backs of chairs come in many different shapes (see p. 70), but certain common types recur, and can be bought singly. They will be much cheaper collected like this, than bought in sets of six or more. Some chairs which were originally caned, will be found

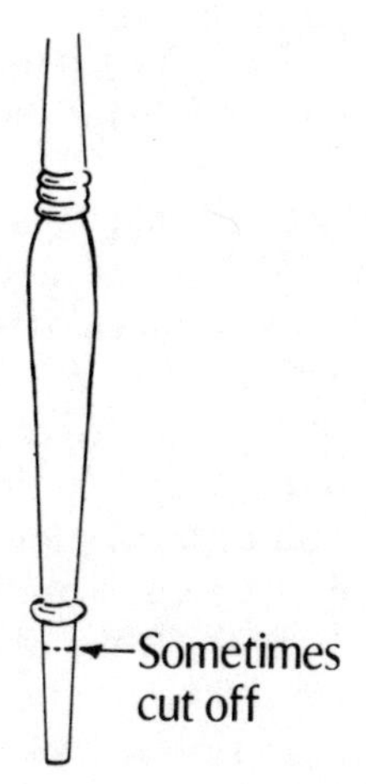

Fig 8

with plywood seats nailed over them. You will see the caning holes if you look at the underside of the seat. You can have these recaned, or upholster the whole of the seat. If the caning is intact on one of a set of chairs and you want to preserve it, you will have to strip them all with chemical stripper. Caustic soda and excessive wetting are not good for cane, and all chairs in a set should really be stripped by the same method to keep the colour uniform.

The top rail of a chair will give you a very good idea of what you will find under the paint or varnish. Everyday wear and tear will have worn away most of the coating, and the colour of the wood will show through. If it looks red, it probably has a bottom layer of the brown paint which leaves a penetrating red stain. This is a bore to remove (see p. 52), but providing the other chairs in your set are warm or dark brown, it can be stained to match.

Cupboards

The most noticeable feature of a cupboard is the doors. They may be tongue-and-groove boarding, flat, or panelled. The first will certainly be pine, but the last two may be partly plywood. Check this by looking at the inside of the doors. Thin flat panels are usually plywood, especially if they are warped, bowed or 'bubbly'. Pine is cut thicker for stability, and the edges of a solid wood panel are bevelled to fit into the frame. Plywood panels are not desirable, but they can be disguised (see Chapter 7). One real advantage is that you will pay less for the piece than for one of solid wood.

Check that the mouldings are intact, as these are a problem to repair or replace. You will have to get them matched by a carpenter, unless you are one yourself. It is unlikely that you will find modern mouldings to match, and in any case these are usually made of ramin, not pine. Occasionally a top moulding can be completely removed without altering the look of the piece too much. Figure no. 19 on page 66 shows one such cupboard. As for chests of drawers, knobs, handles and locks can be replaced; likewise hinges, both steel and brass.

Don't forget that cupboards can be adapted to many uses. The doors can be salvaged from a rickety frame, and a new one built, or ugly doors can be discarded and the cupboard used without, as a bookcase. For more ideas, read Chapter 6 on Adaptations.

Washstands

You are most likely to come across the washstands which have tiled backs, and these tiles are easily changed, if you don't like them. The sort of washstand that has a frame round the sides is older, and the legs are usually prettier and lighter than on the

Fig 9

tiled ones (figure 9). Sometimes there is a hole in the top for a basin, and I think these look nicest with a basin set in, if you happen to have one.

Washstands are immensely useful. They can serve as writing tables, dressing tables, bathroom sink units, side tables, etc. The one likely problem is water stains. Very bad ones may not disappear completely, but they can be lessened by treatment with oxalic acid (page 55).

These pointers should be some help in assessing an unstripped piece of furniture, but after a while your own developing taste and judgement will be the best guide. Don't overface yourself when you begin – start with something small to get your hand in. Ideally, try to strike a balance between paying a great deal for a piece of furniture which may turn out to be a mistake, and putting a lot of work into something cheap which is not worth the effort. Always ask yourself the two questions: Do I need it? Do I really like it? If the answer to either is no, then it will probably sit in your garage or shed for years – a silent reproach.

3 · Stripping

To strip or not to strip

Before starting to strip a piece of furniture, look at it carefully. Do you really want to strip it? Many old finishes add to the value of a piece. Obviously a faded mahogany table with a huge black water mark is a disaster, but it is the water mark that is the problem, not the fading. Any table which has been used for a hundred or more years will inevitably collect a haze of scratches, dents or patchy marks. If it is also glowing with wax and loving care, these marks will blend into a general effect of mellowed age.

Pine furniture appears under many disguises. Most common is a coat of ordinary modern gloss paint. Occasionally, however, one meets a piece of pine furniture which still has its original coat of blue or green milk paint, probably fairly shabby. This paint was made by mixing coloured pigments, like iron oxide, into a base of buttermilk or skim milk, and it is a hard and penetrating finish. Many people collect the furniture which has these old colours, and they command high prices especially in the United States, but increasingly in England. Before you decide to strip it, try washing it in a mild soap solution and then giving it a coat of wax. You may be pleasantly surprised. The same advice goes for painted bedroom furniture which is decorated with fake bambooing or lines of 'striping' or 'lining' around drawers and frame. An antique finish may be in good condition except for a hopelessly damaged top, for instance, in which case you may be able to paint this section only, copying the old design. Read *The Pauper's Homemaking Book* (a Penguin paperback) or *Paint Magic*, both by Jocasta Innes, for excellent information on old and new painting techniques. In Chapter 7 I have described some that I have tried, and found much easier than I expected.

BASIC RULES

If your painted finish is not a valuable antique one, and you want to strip it, there are several methods. There are also certain rules to be observed, and they apply no matter what restoration or removal work you are doing. Some may seem ridiculously obvious, but I still have to force myself to follow them; putting down newspaper, for instance. In the enthusiasm of wanting to get started, I tend to have a little 'dabble', just to see how it is going to go. Several hours later I find myself faced with a major cleaning job, not to mention ruining clothes and perfectly good rubber gloves. Here are my rules. I won't mention them every time they are appropriate in the course of instructions, because this adds confusion, and makes the whole process seem more complicated than it is.

1 Work in a well-ventilated area – ideally outdoors. Many strippers give off toxic fumes.

2 Put down lots of newspapers, especially if you are working indoors. If it looks like being a damp job, put a layer of polythene (such as a bin-liner bag, torn open) under the newspapers. You will need extra sheets of newspaper on the side, for scraping the softened goo onto. If you scrape it onto the newspaper you are using as the underlay, you will almost certainly kneel in it later on.

3 Wear old clothes and use rubber gloves which you keep for messy jobs or are prepared to relegate to same afterwards.

4 When using a non-caustic stripper, take off any handles or knobs. It seems a bore when you want to get on with the job, but it is a greater bore to try to clean and scrape round them. It generally takes only a few moments' work with a screwdriver, and they can be soaking in their own cleaner while you get on with the stripping.

5 **Do everything with the grain.** This means scraping, sanding, and putting on varnish, sealer or polish. The moment you are tempted to have a little scrape across the grain will be the moment the tool sinks into the wood. The only exception is when sanding the spindles of a turned leg, when you really have to go across the grain to get into the grooves.

6 If you are matching new wood to old, do any colour testing on an inconspicuous part of the new piece, because stain, once applied, is difficult to remove. To check that the old and new will

match when finished, lick your finger and dab on both. This gives a good idea of what the wood will look like when polished.

METHODS OF STRIPPING

There are two basic methods of stripping: using caustic soda or using commercial paint stripper. All the firms which do large-scale stripping use one or other form of these two methods, though they have optimum conditions and helpful refinements, such as high-pressure hoses and heated tanks. Pine furniture is generally stripped with caustic soda, because it eats quickly through many layers of paint or varnish, and makes a good stab at removing the old milk-based paints. The wood emerges clean and smooth, but too pale for some tastes. In the United States, the vogue for Early American furniture leads to a preference for honey brown and even darker furniture; light coloured pine is more generally popular in England. The use of commercial chemical stripper, such as that available in hardware stores, is preferable for hardwood furniture, because caustic soda roughens up the grain, darkens the wood, and strips it of its character as well as varnish. The professionals use chemical stripper in large quantities, and there is a firm called 'Dip 'n Strip' which immerses its furniture in a whole vat of it. If I am stripping anything small, I use a gel form of a chemical stripper, and it is also useful for things which cannot be wetted (like the legs of an upholstered chair), or those having only a layer of varnish. Pine pieces which do not fit into these categories, I strip with caustic soda (lye, in the USA), in one of two forms.

Caustic soda stripping

Caustic soda (Sodium Hydroxide granules) is sold in tins for cleaning drains. I have two ways of using it, which I call Hot and Cold. 'Hot' because when you add caustic soda to water, it boils up into a strong hot solution which you put *onto* the wood. The 'Cold' refers to my bath, where I use large quantities of more diluted caustic soda, and immerse my furniture in it.

Before describing the two processes, I would like to dispel some of the myths surrounding caustic stripping. I imagine it is the legends of bodies being dissolved in tanks that have made people fear it, but I have used caustic soda for years without the slightest trouble, and would far rather work with it than with methylated spirits. Of course it is corrosive and potentially dangerous, but then so is chemical paint stripper. Both burn if you get them on your skin, or in your eyes, but both can be washed off with water. If you wear strong, chemical resistant rubber gloves, and sunglasses to protect your eyes, you will come to no harm.

Some people fear that their piece of furniture will come to bits in a tank of caustic soda. It will, if you leave it in too long. On the other hand, long soaking in clean water, or even rain, will also dissolve old glues. The important thing is to be careful, and keep an eye on the stripping once you have started. If you are a keen collecter of pine furniture, you will have come across many pieces which look dry and white, and which are beginning to show a crystalline deposit on the surface. This is all due to *bad* stripping with caustic soda, and these over-stripped and under-neutralized pieces are main contributors to caustic soda's poor reputation. In my instructions I have tried to point out the pitfalls which give rise to disappointing results. Be comforted with the thought that very few mistakes are irredeemable.

HOT CAUSTIC

Hot caustic is more concentrated than cold, and is therefore more dangerous. Keep some plain water nearby, and wash any spills off directly. To protect my arms, I usually wear a pair of ordinary rubber gloves, the longest I can find, inside the chemical resistant ones. These catch some of the dribbles that inevitably run down your arms when you are working upwards – on a tall cupboard, for instance. You need gum boots, too, because the hosing down process involves you in a lot of water. I will list all the equipment you need, and then give an outline of the method for quick reference, followed by an elaboration to clarify some details. Here is what you will need. (If you are going shopping you might at the same time like to check the finishing lists on pages 44 and 47.)

- A small tin of caustic soda, from a chemist or hardware store (or several, to strip a large object)

- A large pack of 0 steel wool, or a small pack and some Scotchbrite scourers
- A scraper and a shavehook
- A large container of malt vinegar
- Wallpaper paste (cold water starch)
- Thick rubber gloves (chemical resistant, like Northands, and preferably the gauntlet type, not fabric-cuffed)
- Sunglasses, or spectacles if you happen to wear them
- Rubber boots and old clothes
- A mixing bowl (not aluminium), or plastic bucket

The method is as follows:

1 Pour a pint of cold water in the mixing bowl, and stir in about a tablespoon of wallpaper paste. Put on your gloves, and then add half a tin of caustic soda to the mixture, till it bubbles up. The bowl should feel very hot. *Never* add the water to the caustic soda, because it spits.

2 Put the object you are stripping out of doors where you do not want to see anything grow again. Best of all, over a drain. Put on your glasses. Use a wad of steel wool (or a cotton mop) to apply the caustic mixture to the object. The wallpaper paste stops it running off or dripping. Leave it for half an hour to an hour, and check with a scraper to see if the caustic has softened all the paint layers. If it has, then:

3 Still wearing glasses, hose the piece of furniture down, while scrubbing along the grain with wire wool or the Scotchbrite scourer. Hot water encourages the working of the caustic. Repeat if necessary.

4 When all the paint is off, hose it down well, inside and out, and let it dry – at least superficially.

5 Neutralize the caustic soda (alkali) with undiluted vinegar (acid). Pour the vinegar into a bowl, and using a sponge or cloth, slosh a good deal of vinegar all over the piece, making sure that it gets into every crevice, inside and out. This is *most* important. If the caustic is not neutralized, it will appear later as a crystalline deposit on the surface.

6 Let it get really dry before applying any finish. Don't try to rush this by placing it too near direct heat, or parts of it may

warp or split. In a normal living room, a chest of drawers, say, should dry out in three or four days. Outdoors, you need to allow a good week.

This is the basic process, and is most effective in *hot* weather; it doesn't work at all well in the cold. After you have applied the solution, try to leave it alone for at least the time I have recommended (30 to 60 minutes), before checking it. The time it takes for the caustic to get down to bare wood depends on the number of layers, and what they are, but you will know it is working when the paint changes colour and becomes soft. If the caustic starts to dry out before it has got through the paint, sprinkle some hot water on it to keep it active. Impatience does not pay, because if patches which have already come clean have then to sit under further coats of the caustic solution, they will become slightly darker than the rest. Don't panic if this happens, however, because the effect can be minimised later, and will in any case become less noticeable after a while. I once stripped a large cupboard in cold caustic in my bath, and left it tipped in the solution overnight, by mistake. As a result, I was left with a long diagonal mark right across it, with one half darker than the other. This effect was rather obvious for about a year, despite my camouflage attempts, but it has now vanished.

Be careful when working with scrapers and shavehooks. They are useful for getting into crevices and mouldings, where the paint is always thickest, but can make nasty gouges if you are careless. Pine is a soft wood, and particularly vulnerable when wet. Be very strict with yourself about working with the grain, and don't dig too hard with the point of the tool. For a turned leg, a good tip is to wrap some steel wool around a piece of string. This can be worked around the spindles the way you dry your back with a towel.

COLD CAUSTIC

If you think you will be doing a lot of stripping, it is worthwhile setting up a bath or tank of the caustic solution, as it can be used over and over. In my case it is literally a bath, complete with feet and taps. Because it is very old fashioned, it is much narrower at one end, and deeper near the taps. This is a bore, as most furniture is squarish, and I always have problems fitting it in. A galvanized tank of the sort used to catch rainwater would really be better, and in fact any solid container will do, but not aluminium, because it reacts with caustic.

Set your bath up where no child can get at it. I have a heavy old door which I lay over mine when it is not in use. As I can hardly lift it myself, it is a pretty good security measure. In fact there is more of a danger of drowning than of burns from the caustic.

Fill your container with cold water. I buy my caustic soda from an agricultural merchant, in six kilo tubs. One of these normally makes a strong enough solution for my bath, in *hot* weather. I had to renew it recently, and because it was nearly October, could not get the caustic to work properly without using two tubs. (If you plan to do a lot of stripping, or have a friend who will share it, the cheapest way is to buy a bulk supply from Fiddes of Cardiff.) As a general guide, the proportions you need are 1 oz. of caustic soda to 1 gallon of water. Measure out the water first, and then tip in the caustic soda granules and stir them with a stick. (You don't need wallpaper paste because you will be putting the furniture into the solution, not the solution onto the furniture.) Now put the object you are stripping into the bath. From this point the process is much the same as for hot caustic, except that you leave the furniture in for two or three hours. Check it now and then to see how it's doing, and when the paint is hanging in tatters from the immersed part, remove the whole thing from the bath and hose it down. As you hose, scrub the paint off with steel wool or a Scotchbrite scourer. With luck, this section will now be down to the bare wood. Even if it is not, replace the piece in the bath with a new part down. You can return to the other later.

One unforeseen problem is that wood floats. This means that you put in a table and it bobs up to the surface, usually turning over to expose the section that you want immersed. You have to use bricks and weights of all kinds to keep the things underwater. If you have several pieces in at once, sometimes you can wedge them against each other. The only advantage to this buoyancy is that you can never lose any blocks or other bits that come unglued. They simply drift up from the murky depths and can be rescued for reglueing. Glass and putty are quite unharmed by caustic. This makes it a useful way of stripping old windows. Mirror glass, on the other hand, must *not* go in, because the silvering will be ruined. In any case, mirrors are usually quite easy to remove from their frames. There is also no need to remove hinges or brass fittings in this kind of stripping, unless they are in the way. In fact it is quite a useful method of cleaning them too.

Pine dealers who strip their own furniture with caustic, generally heat their baths. This means that the process is greatly speeded up, and that the wood is not saturated. A good professional stripper works over the pieces while they are in the tank, so that they are usually in and out within the hour. If pine is left to soak for ages, particularly in a heated bath, most of the life goes out of it with the paint. When dry it will have to be carefully neutralized to make sure that the acid soaks in as deeply as the caustic will have done. This kind of over-stripping can leave pine looking white and parched, but even such pieces are not beyond redemption. In Chapter 8 I have described how I dealt with a blanket box that was in a very bleached condition.

I would not recommend caustic soda to anyone wishing to strip hardwoods, like elm, oak and mahogany. Apart from the darkening and roughening effect that I have already mentioned, furniture made of these woods does not lend itself to being soaked. The wood will swell, old joints may come apart, and veneers will lift and blister. (A veneer is a thin layer of decorative wood applied to a solid carcase, usually of a cheaper wood.) In addition, by subjecting a fine piece of hardwood furniture to caustic soda, you will take away the antique surface, or patina, which it has taken years to achieve. The one exception I make to the hardwood rule is kitchen chairs, which are usually made of beech and elm. If they have only one coat of varnish, I strip them by hand with a chemical stripper, but I am really defeated by the legs of these chairs, when covered with layers of paint. I would rather subject them to the caustic, and sand down the roughness later. I do try to strip them quickly with little soaking, so that they do not become too dark or fluffed up.

Eventually a caustic bath will need renewing, either because it has become diluted by rainwater, or because you want to make a fresh start. You empty the bath by siphoning – *not* directly from the bath, but by filling a five or six foot length of hosepipe with clean water. Holding a finger over both ends of the hose, to keep the water in, put one end into the bath. The water will then pour out of the other end, followed by the caustic solution. This will continue to drain away as long as you keep the bath end of the hose submerged, and the other end below the level of the bath.

Commercial chemical stripping

If you have a piece of furniture covered with layers of paint or gummy varnish which is not suitable for caustic stripping, you must now prepare to strip it with a commercial paint remover. (If you have only one layer of varnish, first read the section on Revivers in this chapter, on page 36.) Many people will have noticed that there are several new products on the market claiming to strip ten or more coats in one go. My attempts to use them are all described in Chapter 8. To use one of the traditional strippers, you will need the following supplies:

- A tin or bottle of paint stripper (any, but I like Blackfriars)
- Steel wool (0 and a coarser one – perhaps no. 2 or 3)
- Rubber gloves
- A wide scraper
- Newspapers
- A paint brush (you can use one that has hardened with old paint; by the end of the stripping it will be soft)
- A dish, bowl or jar into which to decant some of the stripper

Set yourself up on the newspapers, and pour some of the stripper into the extra jar. I generally use a gel-type of paint stripper, because it stays on vertical surfaces and doesn't drip.

Dip your brush into the stripper, and paint over one section of the piece of furniture. In a few moments, dab a second coat rather thickly over the first. The mixture will soon begin to bubble, and you can scrape it off. For this you can use the metal scraper, or coarse wire wool, followed by medium (0). Try both, to see which works best for you. In either case, you need lots of spare newspaper to receive the goo. The stripper only works while it is wet so, to prolong its action if you have many layers to remove, cover it with strips of plastic food-wrap. You may find you need several applications of stripper to remove every trace of paint or varnish.

When one section is clear, start on the next. Attack carved

mouldings and crevices with an old toothbrush, a wooden manicure stick, a vegetable brush, or anything else which will not damage the wood.

For my final clean up, I use 0 or 00 steel wool. (A word of caution here: if you are planning on staining your piece of furniture, take care that you do not 'polish' the wood by rubbing it too hard with *fine* steel wool. This will prevent the stain from soaking in evenly. If you suspect that this has happened, sand the whole thing down to remove any shine.)

At the end of the stripping, read the instructions on your tin or bottle of stripper, in case there is another step. Sometimes you are required to wash off any residue with water, but more often you are now ready to move on to Finishing (Chapter 4). One consolation for the labour involved in chemical stripping is that there is no waiting for the piece to dry out, unless you have been forced to use water.

Dip 'n Strip

I mentioned earlier a franchise concern called Dip 'n Strip who immerse objects in a vat of chemical stripper. I have listed their present addresses in the back of the book, and if there is a branch near you, it is well worth considering for pieces of furniture that are too large for you to handle, or covered in more layers than you can face. Using chemicals, they can handle hardwoods and even veneered furniture, without raising the grain or affecting the wood. It is certainly more expensive than a tin of paint stripper, but a good deal less so than some of the new products. If there were a branch in my area, I would use it for chairs and other turned items, which I really hate to strip, and for anything intricate made of hardwood. Doors, especially house doors, can be awkward. They are rather heavy to manoeuvre in a caustic soda bath – they don't actually fit in mine. These can be taken to a professional caustic stripper, or to Dip 'n Strip. The former is considerably cheaper, but the door will take longer to dry out. Before committing anything to a professional stripper, look around to see if the pieces of furniture standing in his yard are in good condition. If he is using caustic soda, and they are dry and showing signs of crystalline deposit, he may be leaving them in too long.

Other methods

Revivers are really a way of avoiding stripping. If you have only one layer of dirty varnish on a piece of furniture, first try rubbing in a reviver with 00 steel wool. Use Colron's Restorer and Cleaner, or make one yourself by mixing

- one part raw linseed oil
- one part vinegar
- one part methylated spirits (denatured alcohol)

Apply the reviver gently, working with the grain, and wipe up the surface with rags. When it is clean, there should be just enough of the old finish left to form a base for waxing.

Methylated Spirits Also known as 'wood alcohol' and 'denatured alcohol'. It dissolves French polish and certain varnishes very effectively. Pour a little on the surface of the wood, and scrub it in with 0 or 00 wire wool. Then wipe off the dissolved polish with rags or newspaper. The fumes are unpleasant and toxic, so work in a very well-ventilated room. When the old finish is off, you can apply a new one immediately, because the meths evaporates almost as you apply it.

Ammonia You can try using household ammonia, but ideally obtain the *pure* kind ('910' or '880') from Fiddes (p. 96) or large chemists. This will strip old polish and varnish, and also the old refractory milk paints. The method for using ammonia is on page 52, but I would emphasize that the fumes are *extremely* unpleasant. Work out of doors.

Washing Soda A strong hot solution of washing soda (Sodium Carbonate) will remove French polish. It is also very useful as a final scrubbing rinse after stripping with caustic soda, because it removes any grey or dirty residue in the wood. As long as any caustic has been neutralized, there is no need to do it again for washing soda – just rinse well.

Blow-torch This is not recommended because of the risk of scorching the wood. Even if you plan to repaint your door afterwards, someone else in a future generation may want it bare. It is very discouraging to get to the end of a stripping enterprise and find old scorch marks.

Scrapers and shavehooks

A cabinet scraper is a small flat oblong of metal, with very sharp edges. To use it, you hold it upright in both hands, pushing it away from you with your thumbs. This scrapes off a thin shaving of wood, or varnish – or both, if you are unskilled. Scrapers are difficult to use, and whenever I have tried, I have spent most of the time thinking how much easier it would have been to use paint stripper. They are also extremely difficult to sharpen properly and only work on flat surfaces, so a more practicable alternative for our purposes is to use broken glass. Drop an old piece of glass into a bucket to break it, and select a bit with a straight edge. Glass does a good job of scraping, particularly in awkward corners, and you can simply throw away a dull piece and pick up another. It is rather cramping on the hands, however.

A shavehook is a crude alternative to the scraper. It can be drawn or tapped along surfaces, using either the straight or the curved edge, and will often remove old paint right down to the bare wood. I use a shavehook all the time on skirting boards and other indoor fittings.

STRIPPING PAINTWORK FOR DECORATION

I think this is worth a word, because it is one of the most common problems to arise. My general advice on stripping woodwork prior to painting is: don't. Unless you have a caustic tank already in action and are prepared to take doors off their hinges, stripping woodwork is a daunting task. Of course there are occasions when the old paint is in such a terrible, flaky condition that you have no alternative. Before resorting to strippers, take a shavehook and try drawing the *convex* side down the paint. It will often come away in great flakes, leaving a layer of primer or bare wood. I scraped all the paint off some door panels in a few moments this way.

I find that some sections of the woodwork are more vulnerable to chipping than others, and one of these is the curved edge of a door frame, where the latch is. Again, I take my shavehook, and this time run the *concave* edge down the whole length of the moulding. I don't let myself be drawn onto the adjoining edges of the frame, because this starts a relentless progression. I give a good rub down with sandpaper or a Quiksand flexible sanding block, and then fill in any chips which have extended onto the flat parts of the frame with fine surface filler. Bare wood and any filled patches need a coat of quick-drying primer undercoat, and then they are ready to receive a topcoat with the rest. This technique of scraping with the concave edge of a shavehook also works very well on the curved tops of skirting boards.

It is possible that you have an entire staircase or panelled hall that you want to strip down to the bare wood: oak, chestnut or another hardwood will have to be stripped with chemical stripper. If it is pine, you may be able to use caustic soda, but it largely depends on the floor underneath, because the rinsing down is quite messy. If I were to strip our staircase, I would certainly try caustic first, using a very thick mixture of the hot caustic, described on page 29. I would take the precaution of taping some polythene sheeting around the bottom to try to keep some of the water off the floor. I have stripped a cottage staircase most successfully with caustic, but the floor at the bottom was concrete which simplified matters. Ronstrip (p. 87) is expensive and messy, but you could try the *hot air stripper* described below, noting my warnings, and practising on something expendable first.

Hot air stripper

This power tool works on the same principle as a blowtorch, but without the flames. You hold it in your hand like an electric drill, and play a stream of hot air over the paint surface, scraping off the softened paint with a shavehook or scraper. It is an efficient stripping tool, and clean to use, because the shavings that fall to the ground are dry and can be swept up like bits of paper. Unfortunately it can still scorch the wood if held too close, so I cannot recommend its use on furniture or valuable panelling. The Black and Decker stripper costs about the same as a power jigsaw, but you can hire one very cheaply. Be wary of powerful industrial models – they work more quickly, but are correspondingly more inclined to scorch.

FLOORS

When it comes to floors, there is really no practicable alternative to sanding. Have it done professionally, or hire a sander for a couple of days. Before you start, to save on sandpaper, go over the floor with a high-powered solvent to remove old polish and wax. Some of the polish people, like Armstrong, sell removers, usually containing ammonia. You apply them liberally to about a four-foot square, leave them for fifteen minutes to work, and then scrub up the resultant mess with a scourer and rinse off. If you cannot find one of these cleaners in the shops, you can get one from a janitorial supply house (look in the Yellow Pages). When you hire a sander, get an edge sander as well – the companies usually do a reduction on the double hire – and lots of sandpaper. Some friends of mine ran out of sandpaper on a Saturday night and had to waste a whole day of hiring. Even with a dustbag, there is a lot of fine dust, so wear a mask and seal your room off from the rest of the house as best you can.

Stripping, especially in a caustic bath, is surprisingly good fun. I am always reluctant to get started, but once I have, I love it. The layers of paint come off in sheets, and as the wood emerges I am spurred on by thoughts of the finished product. Having to let the wood dry out afterwards is a great anticlimax, and I tend to bring unsuitably large objects into the warmth of the kitchen to speed up the process. At last the finishing stage is reached: the final sanding, polishing and waxing.

4 · Finishing

I shall make as many enemies as friends in writing this chapter, because the refinishing of wood is an extremely controversial subject. Should you wax bare wood? Is dirt part of the 'patina' or mellow glow on a much-polished antique? Were varnishes used before the 19th century? Every refinisher has his favourite techniques, and is usually not prepared to consider any others.

Two years ago, a friend of mine bought a set of six kitchen chairs of the scroll-back variety, which had been very badly stripped. They were pale grey, with no trace of polish. She asked the advice of a local cabinet maker, who gave her some reddish-brown French polish. This she applied to a couple of the chairs, and they looked much brighter and warmer – if not a little hot. When she showed them to me, I suggested that the polish would scratch, and indeed a scrape with her fingernail revealed the old grey wood underneath. With some labour she restripped the chairs, and then talked to a local pine dealer. He gave her a runny brownish paste to put on, and again the chairs were much improved in colour. This time we dripped some water onto them, and this took them straight back to the bare wood.

Either of these finishes would have been fine in their place, but neither was the slightest use for family kitchen life. In the end we decided to start by tackling the grey colour itself. We scrubbed it with a hot washing-soda solution and a Scotchbrite pad, and got off buckets of filth. The chairs were now beige instead of grey, so we rinsed them well to remove any soda, and let them dry overnight. A good rub down with sandpaper, followed by a coat of stain, brought them up to more normal chair condition, and we finished with an application of polyurethane varnish, rubbed down with steel wool and waxed.

The chairs were now ready for kitchen use. The finish would survive heavy handling, and an occasional waxing would gradually improve their appearance. This is the treatment I recommend for functional pieces of furniture which are likely to have water, alcohol, or other substances spilt on them. There is another more traditional polish finish for decorative items. I will describe both of these processes, but first you must prepare the surface of the wood to receive them.

SANDING, BLEACHING AND STAINING

Sanding

Don't skimp on this step – it is an important one. The final effect of your finished piece of furniture will largely depend on how much work you put in at this stage.

The word 'sandpaper' is a misnomer, because nowadays abrasive papers are made with tiny particles of glass, aluminium oxide, garnet, or silicon carbide. Glasspaper is cheap, but wears out quickly; the others are more durable, and waterproof silicon carbide paper can be washed and used again. The variety of choice can be confusing, and so can the fact that sandpaper is used for smoothing down surfaces, *and* for keying or roughing them up. To make it all simpler, I will list the grades and qualities of papers that I use for the various processes:

	glasspaper (yellow)	*waterproof silicon carbide* (dark grey)	*equivalent steel wool*
For preparing bare wood:			
Coarse:	M2 (grit 70)	120	1
Medium:	F2 (grit 100)	180	0
Fine:	1 (grit 150)	220	00
For polishing wood after staining, and keying varnished and French polished surfaces for further coats:			
Superfine:	Flour (grit 240) (pale grey)	400	000 & 0000

To prepare the wood, I start with a medium paper and then move on to a fine. The reason for not using the superfine papers and steel wool at this stage is that they polish the wood so much that the fibres cannot accept a stain, and it will go on unevenly. Never use worn-out coarse sandpaper in the belief that it has worn down to medium – some large particles of the abrasive always remain and will scratch the wood.

SANDING TOOLS

There are several gadgets available for making sanding easier, and the simplest of these is a sanding block. Wrap a piece of sandpaper around a solid object like an offcut of wood, a blackboard eraser (which has convenient indentations in the side for your fingers), or a child's building block. You hold this sanding block in the palm of your hand, and it makes a firm back-up to the sandpaper, which is useful on large flat surfaces.

A more flexible kind of block, obtainable from hardware stores, is one called Quiksand. This is actually a firm sponge, coated on four sides with aluminium oxide paper of different grades (I use medium/fine). I find these blocks are a good handy size, and they can be washed and reused.

For preliminary smoothing of the crevices in a turned leg, use a half-round file, then move on to sandpaper.

Three useful tools which fit onto an electric drill are an 'orbital' or 'finishing' sander, a 'drum' sander, and a 'flapwheel'. These can all be used with the grain, but the orbital sander has a barely perceptible circular action, and should be followed by hand sanding to erase any swirl marks. The flapwheel consists of little flaps of abrasive paper which flick the wood; as the tips of the flaps wear down, new paper is exposed. It comes in various sizes, and I find the smallest one particularly useful on curved surfaces and turned legs.

One drill attachment that should never be used on bare wood is a disc sander, because it leaves circular marks so difficult to remove, that you would be better off doing the job by hand in the first place. Remember that stain and polish will highlight any sanding errors.

To make certain that you have got your wood really smooth, you can wipe a damp cloth over the surface. This will reveal any scratches that are left and will also raise the grain slightly, so that a final sanding will leave it ultra-smooth. Because pine is a soft wood, it is quite easy to sand smooth, but there are one or two trouble spots. Chief of these is turned items, especially chair legs. There is really no alternative to sanding *around* the spindles, thereby going across the grain which always runs up and down a leg. Use fine sandpaper to minimize scratches, and as a final touch, wrap a piece of the sandpaper around the leg, and cupping your hand over it, give the leg a good polish up and down.

Inner surfaces, like the cubbyholes of a desk, or the curved edges under a plinth, can also be awkward to sand. For these, I make my piece of sandpaper into a small pad, and use the tips of my fingers to apply firm pressure to it.

Sanding wood is a tedious process, but the next steps in finishing furniture go very quickly and are more rewarding. When you are satisfied with your sanded surface, lick your finger and dab it on the wood to get a rough approximation of what it will look like when polished. Do you like the colour? If you do, you can skip the next section and go to page 45 for finishes. Otherwise, read on.

Bleaches and stains

Perhaps your wood has been darkened by caustic soda, or is simply a dingy colour that you don't like. In either case you can change it, though you will probably find, as many people do, that you will like your wood darker and darker as time goes on. I used to try everything to get my pine to a pale gold colour, but now I much prefer the dark honey-brown of old school desks.

BLEACHES

To lighten your wood, the simplest bleach to try first is ordinary Parozone or household bleach, used full strength. Pour some into a bowl and apply it generously with a cloth or sponge, *with good ventilation*. To emphasize this last point, I have a cautionary tale: a couple of years ago I decided to bleach a cupboard that I had just stripped (I was still in my Pale Pine phase), so I carried it upstairs to the bathtub. Working in a rather small bathroom with the windows shut, I bleached away happily, unaware of any fumes because my nose was blocked up with a cold. After about twenty minutes, I found that I was having some trouble breathing, and a short while later I was in the middle of an attack of asthma. I made a futile search for my husband's asthma inhaler, and when he got home he found me kneeling by an open window, gasping at the fresh night air. I'm sorry to say that he was amused by my story (when I was able to tell it), and said that chlorine was extensively used as a poison gas in the First World War.

If you find that one or two applications of household bleach are not enough to get the paleness you want, there are proprietary two-part bleaches on the market – Rustins make one – which have a much more drastic effect. They remove the natural colour from the wood, and are used to achieve finishes like bleached mahogany. Follow the instructions supplied with the bleach.

Oxalic acid, used in a 'saturate solution', that is to say with crystals added to water till no more will dissolve, is a powerful bleach for small black marks. I have described how to use it on p. 55.

If you find that your piece of furniture has dark patches where some caustic soda solution has lain too long, you can either bleach the dark sections with a cloth dipped in household bleach, or stain the pale bits to match the dark.

STAINS

There are many kinds of stain on the market, all soluble in different mediums such as oil, spirit or water. I have found that the penetrating stains which are generally sold as Wood Dyes are simple to use and work well. They do not raise the grain of the wood, and all the shades in a range can be mixed to give a greater variety of colours. Blackfriars and Colron produce ranges of wood dyes; I will list the colours I use in each. The names are misleading, and Teak made by Colron is a much darker and redder colour than the Blackfriars Teak. Don't be tempted by a Colron stain called Yellow Pine – they really do mean yellow. For pine and beech, I use either

Blackfriars Wood Dye, colours: *Teak* and *Medium Oak* (the latter for mixing to obtain darker shades)

or

Colron Wood Dye, colours *English Light Oak* and *Medium Georgian Oak* (for mixing).

If you only want to buy one stain, then I recommend Blackfriars' Teak. It is a warmer tone than Colron's English Light Oak, and gives an excellent antique pine colour.

To apply the stain you need some cloths or paper towels. The method is as follows:

1 Decide which inconspicuous part of your piece of furniture is going to be your test area.

2 Shake the tin of Teak or Light Oak stain, and with a cloth, spread a little of it over a patch of bare wood in the test area. Give it a few seconds to dry slightly, then lick your finger and dab it on the stained bit to get an idea of the polished result. Is it dark enough? If not, pour some of the stain into a saucer or any container, and add a little of the darker colour of the same brand (don't mix Colron and Blackfriars together). Try out this new colour by the same patch method, and keep adding drops of the darker colour till you achieve an effect that you like.

3 Apply this colour to the whole piece of furniture. The stain can be poured directly from the tin onto the cloth if you are using it as it is. Wipe the stain on with long strokes, using a generous amount. Try not to let the impregnated cloth rest heavily on one spot, because this can cause a dark patch. If this happens, wipe the patch hard with a clean cloth dipped in white spirit, and then go over the whole area again.

4 Let it dry for as long as instructed on the tin. You can apply a second coat if you are not satisfied with the colour. If you are, then you are ready for the next stage.

SEALERS AND WAXING

I do not believe in putting wax directly onto bare wood, although it is a common practice with pine dealers. Wax attracts dirt, and with no protective surface underneath, both wax and dirt will sink deep into the fibres of the wood, which will eventually look dark and muddy. In addition, wax has no resistance to water, spirit or any other stains. Far from building up a gleaming wax surface, you are more likely to be scrubbing it with scouring pads to get rid of grime. What I recommend is a wax finish applied *over* a sealer coat of either varnish or French polish (shellac), depending on the function of your piece of furniture.

Finish for decorative pieces

By decorative, I mean such items as corner cupboards, bookcases, occasional tables that will never have a drink placed on them, etc. Here is what you need:

- A small new bottle of White French Polish or shellac (it has a short shelf life)
- A brush (two inches or so wide), or a cloth
- Methylated Spirits (denatured alcohol), to clean the brush
- Steel wool (preferably 000, but 00 will do in a pinch)
- A good paste wax (any, but see p. 50 for recommendations)

What you are going to do is seal the wood with a coat of French polish (shellac). By this I do not mean that you are going to apply a professional French polished finish with its traditional glassy surface, but just one coat, put on with a brush. Here is how:

1 Vacuum the surface or wipe it over well to remove any dust and grit.

2 Decant some of the French polish into an old jar or dish, and dipping your brush in, spread it over the wood, along the grain. It dries very quickly, and ridges may build up along your stroke lines, but they can be smoothed out later. If it looks really messy, rub it down well with fine sandpaper and apply another coat. You can also spread the polish on with a cloth, pouring a little onto it directly from the bottle. It goes on more thinly this way, and you will probably need two coats.

3 Allow this coat of polish to dry hard (about three hours, or less in a warm room). At this stage it will look patchy, shiny and synthetic.

4 Take a piece of steel wool, dip it into your wax, and rub it well into *every inch* of the surface of the polish, thereby dulling the shine. When you have rubbed over all the surfaces and left a thin film of wax, leave it to harden for about twenty minutes.

5 Then, with a soft duster or cloth, buff the wax by rubbing it vigourously till a sheen appears, and all trace of smear has vanished.

6 Apply a second coat of wax, with a cloth this time. When this layer is polished, you should have a gleaming surface indistinguishable from a plain waxed surface. You can apply more coats of wax until you are satisfied with the shine, but be careful not to leave any smears between coats. A tacky surface will attract and collect dirt.

This finish is good-looking but utterly useless against heat, water or alcohol, so you will need an alternative.

Finish for functional pieces

The polish and wax finish that I have just described is obviously going to be no use on a kitchen table, because spills and marks of all kinds will cut straight through it to the bare wood. If you are an enthusiastic cleaner you could go for a scrubbed table top (see p. 93), but otherwise you want a surface that will repel food, water, alcohol, felt tip pens, etc. The only way to achieve this is to apply a varnish. Any varnish will do, except for spar or yacht varnishes, which are formulated to stay pliable and not dry out. All the polyurethanes are fairly similar, and there is a harder lacquer finish which I will deal with separately.

Anyone who has applied varnish to pine furniture will know that it can cause a colour change in the wood, darkening it to an oily orange colour. To avoid having this happen, first test the varnish on the underside of your surface to see the effect, and if you don't like it, apply a coat of sealer. For this I have used white French polish or shellac, even though it is forbidden by most varnish manufacturers. I wipe on one coat, rub it down when dry with fine steel wool, and apply two coats of varnish on top. This has always worked perfectly well for me, but to be on the safe side, use a *sanding sealer* instead. Joy-plane make one, and you can telephone or write to them for stockists (Tunbridges Ltd, 72 Longley Rd, London SW17, Tel: 01-672 6581).

To apply a varnish finish, you need:

- A tin of sanding sealer (as described above)
- A tin of gloss polyurethane varnish
- A cloth or some rags
- A brush (two inches or so wide)

- Steel wool (00 or 000 grade)
- White spirit (to clean the brush)

1 Apply a coat of sanding sealer if the polyurethane darkens the wood.

2 Let the sealer dry for two or three hours, then rub all over lightly with steel wool. Vacuum the surface or dust it off well.

3 With the brush, apply a coat of polyurethane varnish.

4 When dry, rub it down really well with 00 or 000 steel wool, and apply another coat of varnish.

5 You can apply more coats of varnish if you are dealing with something like a kitchen table, which will receive heavy wear. Four is enough for any surface. Finish with a rub down with steel wool to take away the glassy shine. The matt and satin varnishes are not as hard as the gloss, and you will get a better result by rubbing down a gloss finish.

6 Brush one coat of varnish on the underside of tables to prevent warping.

7 You can apply a wax coating over the varnish to give a soft sheen.

Acid catalyst lacquer (or plastic coating)

This is the last word in the finish world. It works on the same principle as an epoxy glue: you mix the two parts together, and one acts as a hardener on the other. I have used a lacquer called Plastic Coating by Rustins, but not many hardware stores stock it and you may have to put in a special order.

The advantage of this type of coating is that it is even harder and tougher than ordinary ones and is exceptionally resistant to heat. If you give your kitchen table several coats of the lacquer finish it should still show little sign of wear after several years. Saucepans from the Aga can be put directly onto it and in fact it will be more practical than Formica countertops. I suggested to some friends who were building wooden cupboards into their kitchen, that they use pine counter tops finished with a similar two-part varnish. This they did, to the disgust of their builder, who insisted on a piece of Formica next to the sink. Two years later this is stained and scratched, while the wooden surfaces are unscathed.

The method of applying this lacquer is the same as for any polyurethane, except that the two parts have to be mixed together. Don't mix more than you need for one coat, because it won't keep. The proportions vary from make to make, so measure it out in the following way: I take an old jar and pour a measured amount of water into it (representing the lacquer base) marking this level on the outside of the jar. Then add the next measured amount of liquid (representing the hardener), and mark the new level on the jar. When I have poured the water away, I have a disposable jar marked with lines to show how much to add of each of the two parts. I apply the lacquer with a cloth and then throw it away. To clean brushes you need to buy a special solvent, so I don't use them.

One word of caution: This lacquer smells really terrible, and I strongly advise doing the applications in an unused room with the window open. It is advisable to rub each coat down lightly to remove any lumps or bits of grit that may have settled while it was drying.

As you can see, there are various protective finishes for pine, ranging from the enamel-like coating of acid catalyst lacquer to the minimum seal of French polish. I try to assess how much wear a piece of furniture is likely to get, and choose my finish accordingly. For example, on a kitchen dresser I would use polyurethane on the counter shelf, and French polish on the rest. On the other hand, if it had cupboard doors in the base that I was constantly opening and shutting, I would polyurethane those too. For a bedroom chest of drawers the polish finish would probably be adequate, *but* if I knew I would be setting down water glasses or cups of tea on the top, then I would polyurethane that. I would rather be practical from the start than have the heartbreak of having to remove a finish down to the bare wood later to get out stains.

Waxes

The common factor in the different finishes I have described is a final coating of wax. If you rub them down well with steel wool and apply several coats of wax, you will find it very difficult to tell one from another, especially after a few years of polishing and care. But which wax should you use?

Beeswax will come to the minds of most lovers of old furniture. It is a good traditional wax, but very soft, and this means that you can never rub it to a really hard, non-smeary finish. For this reason it is usually mixed with other waxes, and best of all with carnauba, a very hard wax made from the leaves of a Brazilian plant.

There are many furniture waxes and polishes on the market, which you could use, including shoe polish and car wax, the difference being in the degree of hardness you can achieve with successive coats. I don't recommend the silicone waxes because they give little protection and can affect some finishes. Some paste waxes you may meet are Briwax, Keil, Harrell's, Colron Finishing Wax and Antiquax, but my two favourites are Rydenor Hard Wax Polish (Rydenor Products, Thirsk, Yorkshire) and Renaissance Micro-Crystalline wax (Picreator Enterprises Ltd., 44 Park View Gardens, London NW4 2PN).

Apply wax polish sparingly with a cloth, and rub it hard along the grain. The heat you create with the friction of your hand will melt the wax into a smooth coating. As a final touch when I have finished polishing, I sometimes *breathe* on the wood and rub it again. The haze of vapour helps me to get a really good shine; I suppose it is a variant of the army spit-and-polish routine.

Don't get carried away and apply too many coats of polish: a heavy build-up of wax obscures the grain of the wood. Once you have a good surface, burnish it occasionally with a clean soft cloth, and when this treatment no longer restores the shine, it is time to apply more wax.

I think you will find that the three finishes I have described work well and will fill all your needs, but for those who are interested, I have described some others in Chapter 8.

5 · Problems and Repairs

All sorts of problems may arise either during or after stripping a piece of furniture. You are dealing with old furniture, whose latent weaknesses can surface under the strain of being stripped, and, in addition, hidden flaws and stains may emerge from under the layers of paint. Most problems have a remedy, but some are too difficult for the amateur to carry out. Where they are simple and require only basic tools, I will describe them. I will begin with the problems that are likely to arise while actually stripping the furniture, specifically when using caustic soda.

During stripping

OBJECT TOO LARGE FOR YOUR CAUSTIC BATH

If you are determined to strip a large object yourself, the only way is to immerse the bits that will fit into your bath, while occasionally sloshing the solution over the rest. In hot weather the dilute solution may strip the central unsubmerged area, but if the caustic is not working efficiently, you may eventually have to use hot caustic on the unstripped sections. The colour of the sections stripped separately will differ, but you can minimize this with stain, and in any case they will merge in time. I have a kitchen door which had a large diamond shape in the middle because I could only get the four corners into my bath, but a year later this patch has vanished. Alternatively you can take the piece of furniture to a dealer and have him strip it in his bath for you, or to a branch of Dip 'n Strip if there is one nearby.

NOTHING HAPPENS

There are several reasons for this, the most common being that it is too cold for the caustic soda to work. You can leave the project till the weather is warmer, or try pouring boiling water over the piece to activate the caustic. If I am anxious to get on with something when the weather is not right, I sometimes add more caustic to the bath, or renew the whole bath after siphoning out the old solution, as described on page 33.

PAINT THAT WON'T SHIFT

In some cases, stripping proceeds very well until an intractable layer of paint is reached. This may be one of the old milk-based paints which can be very difficult to remove. They were made by mixing a coloured pigment like red iron oxide with skim milk or buttermilk. If rubbing with 0 or 1 steel wool does not break through the surface, you will have to try another method. The easiest is to resort to a chemical paint stripper. If this doesn't work, you can use pure ammonia. I have never had to use it myself, but it is obtainable from Fiddes of Cardiff or from some chemists (ask for either 910 or 'point eight-eighty'). It is an unpleasant substance to work with; if you sniff ordinary household ammonia, you will get some idea of the fumes of the pure variety. With good ventilation, and wearing rubber gloves, pour some of the ammonia over the piece of furniture and scrub it in with steel wool. Nothing will happen until you apply a second coat and scrub again. Rinse well.

RED STAIN

Perhaps the paint has all come off, but you are left with a red stain. This is due to the penetrating red pigment used to colour milk paints. It is a beast to remove, but there are several methods you can try. The easiest is to rub it with steel wool and neat household bleach or methylated spirits. If this does not work, make up a hot solution of washing soda, by adding half a pound of the crystals to five pints of hot water. When they have dissolved, pour the solution over the stain, and after about fifteen minutes scrub it with a brush, steel wool or a Scotchbrite pad. Be sure to rinse off every trace of soda at the end.

OBJECT FALLS APART

You have left it too long in the bath, or it was already pretty rickety. The only thing to do is to finish stripping the individual bits, clean off all traces of glue, and when it has dried, put it back together with fresh glue (I use Evo-Stick Resin W, a white woodworking glue).

Chairs are quite easy to put back together with a few improvised cramps, as long as you have enough pieces still joined together so that you can see which leg goes in which hole: they are not interchangeable. When you have glued and assembled the chair legs and rails, wrap a stout piece of rope twice round the legs, knot it, and twist a stick between the two strands to make a tourniquet. When you have twisted it till the rope is really tight, brace the stick against one of the legs to hold it while the assembly dries (figure 10). This makeshift cramp will work on

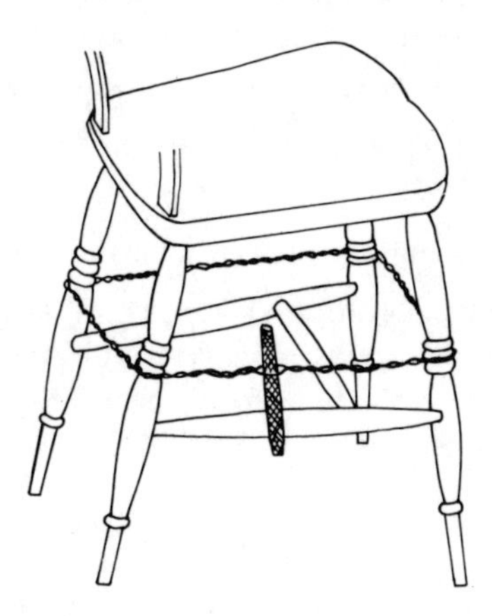

Fig 10

small-to-medium objects, but the carcase of a piece of furniture or a large drawer call for professional sash cramps (figure 11). These are long bars, and a keen handyman friend may have a couple, but if not, take the whole thing to a carpenter.

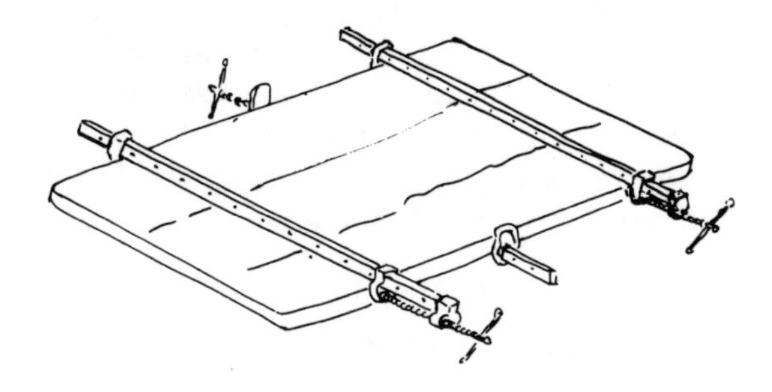

Fig 11

PAINT STUCK IN MOULDINGS

You can scrape the paint out of long mouldings or beading with a shavehook or a pointed stick. Go slowly, because it is easy to slip out of the groove and across a nearby smooth surface. If the mouldings are awkward, leave them to dry. Often the bits of paint will then 'jump' out when tapped or scraped with a sharp tool. If all else fails, use a chemical paint stripper, scrubbing the sections with a toothbrush or plastic vegetable cleaning brush.

PAINT STUCK IN TURNED SECTIONS OF LEGS

Take a long strip of steel wool and wrap it round a piece of string. Then work this around the turnings the way a man dries himself with a towel.

PAINT STUCK IN THE OPEN GRAIN OF HARDWOODS

Paint may lodge in the grain of oak and elm, and steel wool does not dig in far enough to remove it. Try scrubbing the wood with a plastic brush, such as those used for cleaning vegetables, while the object is still wet or a wire brush when it has dried.

After stripping

PATCHES OR STREAKS

This often happens when some parts of the wood have been longer in contact with the caustic solution than others. Bear in mind that the wood will look a bit rough and raw at this stage in any case, particularly if it is fairly modern; the older pieces are usually a smooth mellow colour under the paint. To remedy the patchiness, after you have neutralized the whole thing and let it dry, go over the darker portions with neat household bleach. You can repeat the application if necessary, and if there is still a marked difference go over the *lighter* sections with Colron's light oak stain, or Blackfriars' teak, feathering the edges so that there is no definite line. In any case the discrepancy will become less marked after a few months when the wood has mellowed.

DINGY GREY COLOUR LEFT IN THE GRAIN

A dirty colour sometimes remains in the wood after it has been stripped. Remove it with a strong hot solution of washing soda, scrubbed in with a Scotchbrite scourer or a nylon brush. Be careful to rinse off all the soda solution when you have finished.

RED STAIN

Removal of this stain has been described in the previous section. It is very tedious to deal with, and if slight, can be masked instead with a coat of warm brown stain, such as medium oak.

INK STAINS

Neat household bleach may remove these, but if not you have to use *oxalic acid*, obtainable in powder or crystal form from a chemist. It is a poison, so take care to store it out of reach of children, and wear rubber gloves when using it. Make a saturate solution of the acid by adding the powder to a small container of hot water till no more will dissolve, and brush it on the stain. Let it stand for twenty minutes or so, then wash it off. You can repeat the process several times till you are satisfied, though it is difficult to remove an ink stain completely from pine, because the acid has trouble penetrating the close grain. When you have finished, rinse well, and then wipe the area over with a mild solution of washing soda to remove any traces of the acid.

BLACK WATER MARKS

Same treatment as ink.

MILDEW

Neat household bleach removes mildew from wood most effectively.

FLUFFED UP GRAIN

This happens to hardwoods when they get really wet, and is particularly bad when they have been in contact with caustic soda. The only solution is to sand the whole thing down till it is smooth, starting with medium sandpaper and progressing to fine.

ONE LEG A DIFFERENT WOOD

Because pine furniture was going to be painted, carpenters

sometimes built things with odd pieces of wood that were to hand, or made repairs to an existing piece of furniture with a new bit of a different wood. Sometimes the mismatch doesn't matter: an elm leg with three beech ones is hardly noticeable because the woods are so similar in colour. But occasionally the discrepancy is glaring and hard to live with, like an oak drawer in a pine side table, where the colour and grain of the two woods is totally dissimilar. You can try applying a darkish stain to the whole piece, which will often camouflage the differences, but otherwise you will have to get a new piece made, preferably out of old wood.

WHITE FILLER EVIDENT IN KNOTS, NAIL HOLES, ETC.

This filler is ugly at first sight, but you soon get used to it, as it is one of the common features of stripped pine. If you hate it, dig it out and fill the holes with plastic wood. The natural plastic wood is too pale, so I mix some walnut with it; dark filler is less noticeable than light. Alternatively you can paint the white filler with Artists' oil paints before putting on a coat of sealer or varnish. I match the colour of pine like this: mix together equal blobs of *yellow ochre* and *white*, then add a dash each of *burnt sienna* and *burnt umber*. To make the darker colour of a knot, keep adding burnt umber.

CHIPS AND GOUGES FROM BAD STRIPPING TECHNIQUE

Sometimes these are not your fault; they may be an inheritance from a previous stripper. Old furniture has often gone through many permutations over the years, and it is impossible to predict what lies under the paint and varnish. Whatever the cause, they are difficult to deal with, and you can only go over the surface with sandpaper till they are less noticeable. Pay particular attention to the scrapes or gouges themselves, softening their edges so they blend in better with the surrounding wood. You can fill a deep hole with plastic wood, or glue in a piece of dowel (wooden rod) and paint it to resemble a knot (see above), but remember that slight imperfections will not be so noticeable when the piece of furniture is polished and waxed.

HOLE WHERE A DEAD KNOT HAS FALLEN OUT

Try to avoid this problem by noticing when they are loose and glueing them back in. If they are lost, glue in a piece of dowel, fill any remaining gaps with plastic wood, and paint it as on p. 56.

BURNS

There is no way of restoring burnt wood, though a slight scorch can sometimes be sanded off. If you can't live with the burn mark, paint over it with Artists' oils.

BRUISES AND DENTS

These are surprisingly successfully removed with an ordinary domestic iron. Fold a damp cloth several times and place it over the dent, then lay a warm iron on the cloth for ten minutes or so, lifting it now and then to check progress. The wood will swell as the steam penetrates the fibres. If the wood is polished or varnished, make several slits in the surface with a razor blade along the grain lines, to let the steam through to the wood.

WARPED OR STICKING DRAWERS

Pull the drawer out, and if it is rubbing on the carcase you will see scrape marks along the sides. Try rubbing the sides of the drawers with a candle and this may add enough lubrication to let them move in and out smoothly. If there are no scrape marks, examine the runners. These are strips of wood that the drawer rests on as you pull it in and out (figures 12 and 13). If there are grooves worn in them, fill them with plastic wood or press in a few drawing pins to raise the level. If the runners have been worn down too far for filling, you can glue in a piece of wood, providing that the runner has been worn fairly flat. If not, you will have to chisel it out a bit, which is not an easy job for a beginner. If you are putting in a strip, the easiest thing is to buy a length of ramin from a hardware store. This is the wood sold in strips for picture moulding and general repairs, and is harder than pine. You will be able to choose a piece of the right width and thickness, and then cut it to the correct length. I would glue it with Evo-stick Resin W and hammer in a few panel pins to make sure it holds while the glue sets.

If the runners are not worn, look at the bottom edges of the drawer where they rest on the runners – sometimes these are the culprits. If they are worn down you can glue strips of wood to them by the method I described for runners, as long as the wear is slight, and doesn't reach the drawer bottom. Rub all new wood with a candle.

DRAWER MOVES FROM SIDE TO SIDE WHEN OPENING

If a drawer works unevenly, the guide may be missing. This is a piece of wood outside the runner which keeps the drawer in line (figure 12). If it is worn, you can glue on a strip of wood as described above, or put in a whole new piece if it is missing. Occasionally this problem is due to the carcase of the piece of furniture having gone out of true. To readjust this is beyond the skill of the average handyman.

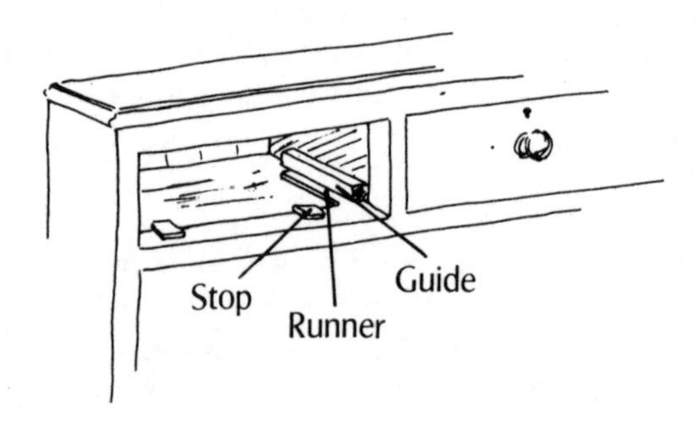

Fig 12

DRAWER GOES IN TOO FAR

This happens because a stop is missing (figure 12). Take out a couple of drawers and look at the framework of the carcase. You will see that the drawers that are working properly are stopped by small thin pieces of wood glued to the rail under them, usually at the front, but occasionally at the back. Replacing them is very simple and satisfying. You glue and pin (with panel pins) two similarly shaped pieces of wood in the gaps left by the old. If you cannot see the marks left by the missing pieces, use the stops on another drawer as a guide as to where to place them.

WHOLE DRAWER HAS DROPPED

The drawer drops because the bottom edges of the sides have

worn right down (figure 13). To get a good repair you have to cut away a section of the drawer side and fit a new piece – not an easy job. Sometimes worn sides will cause a strip to break off the bottom of the *front* of the drawer, and this is even more difficult to repair because of the need to match the grain and colour of the wood.

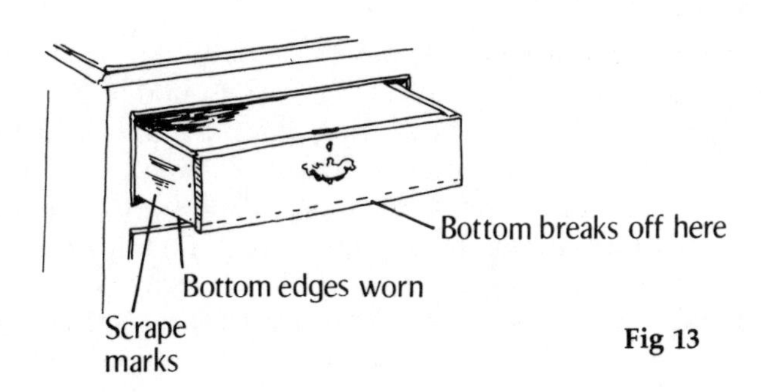

Fig 13

WOBBLY JOINTS

One wobbly joint quickly leads to another, because a piece of furniture is delicately balanced, and each section relies on the stability of its neighbours. If you catch the wobble early, you can often reglue just the one joint, otherwise you will have to take the whole thing apart, scrape off the old glue, and reglue it. If you are dealing with a chair, take care when you are knocking it apart to keep the bits laid out on the floor in their right order, or mark them so they don't get muddled up. 'Taking the whole thing apart' can be more difficult than it sounds. The suspect joints come apart immediately, but others stick fast. Look the piece over carefully for any screws, and remove them. Wrap a thick cloth around the hammer, or put a block of wood between it and the chair, to prevent damage to the wood, then knock against one piece while standing on or holding the adjoining section. If you are dealing with a large piece of furniture like a chest of drawers or a table top, lay a scrap piece of wood in the angle of the joint, and tap your way gently along it, easing it out bit by bit. Too aggressive an attack with the hammer can put strain on the wood and cause splits.

The back of a windsor chair is often a bit loose where it fits into the seat. Don't try to fix this yourself because the uprights are held into the seat with wedges, and the removing and replacing of these is quite a tricky operation. The chairs usually do good service for a long time with wobbly backs. Chair leg assemblies can be held together while the joints dry with a tourniquet made of rope (figure 10).

DOORS BINDING

There are several factors that can cause doors to bind in their frames. In a cupboard, first check that the ground it is standing on is level: if it is not, it may be throwing the framework out of true. The cupboard may have sagged out of shape even if it is on level ground, and in this case the adjustment is not a job for an amateur, because it may involve reassembling the frame.

Loose hinges can cause a door to drop, in which case you need only tighten the screws. Screws are sometimes replaced with larger ones when the originals no longer hold the hinge firmly, and often the heads of the new screws are too large for the countersunk holes in the hinges. If they stand proud of the hinge, they cause it to bind, and you will have to reverse the operation by fitting smaller screws. Unfortunately the old screw holes will now be too big, so glue in some slivers of wood or matchstick to fill them up slightly. To do an even better repair job, fill the old screw holes completely with dowels of the same size, and then drill new pilot holes.

It may be that the hinge itself is worn out. Is there a lot of play in the hinge when you move the door up and down? You can buy replacement hinges, but these are often thinner than the old ones, so insert a piece of card behind the flap to make it up to the right thickness. A hinge should be completely flush with the wood of the door or the frame; if it is recessed, or stands proud of the surface of the wood, it can cause the door to bind.

CRACKS

For long cracks in a table top, the best permanent solution is to remove it from the frame, insert glue in the cracks, and pull it together while it dries. For a large table top you need three sash cramps – long metal bars which will span the whole width (figure 11). A smaller table can be pulled together with a tourniquet, but a wide one would tend to curl up under this treatment. A short crack can be filled with a sliver of wood. Saw along the length of the crack to make it a uniform width, and then glue in a narrow strip of wood. When it has dried you can plane the strip flush with the table top. I couldn't quite face any of this with my own table, so I filled the gaps with plastic wood. This made a temporary repair, but the cracks have opened again.

If you have removed a table top to mend the cracks, don't glue or nail it back in position, because this is what causes the cracks in the first place. When the wood is held rigidly so that it cannot contract or expand, it splits or warps instead. To avoid this, replace the table top with special metal plates that have one wide screw hole (available from Woodfit Ltd, Whittle Low Mill, Chorley, Lancs). These plates let the wood move slightly widthways without splitting (figure 14).

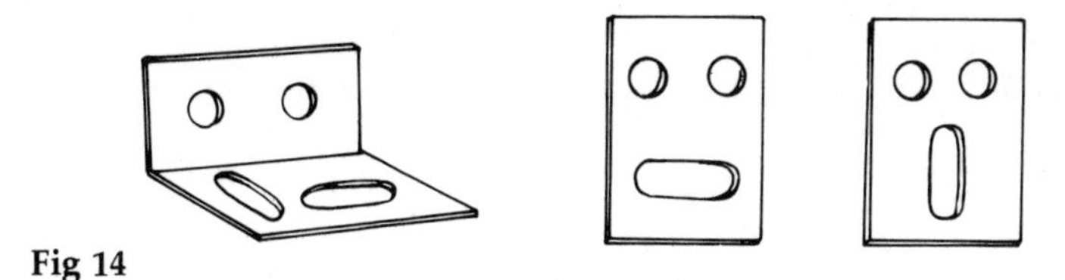

Fig 14

WARPING

This is a problem similar to splitting, due to movement in the wood from atmospheric changes. A table top with the top surface permanently sealed and the underside left bare, is ripe for warping because the underside absorbs moisture from the air and expands, but the top cannot. You should always put one coat of seal or varnish on the underside of a table top or any other large surface that is being refinished.

To treat a warp, you need to remove the affected section from the framework. Wet the hollow, or concave, side by laying it down on damp grass or wet cloths. Then put a weight on top and leave it till the bulge has flattened out. Remove it from its wet resting place and either put it back on its frame and clamp firmly in place till it dries, or lay it on a dry flat area weighted all over until it is quite dry. Prevent it from warping again by sealing both sides when you replace it.

SOUND BUT SAGGY CANING

Saggy cane can sometimes be tightened by a thorough wetting. Leave it in the sun to dry, if possible.

MOULDINGS BROKEN OR MISSING

Replacing a broken moulding should be a simple case of buying a matching piece from among the many mouldings on sale for picture framing and general repairs. When you go to look at these, however, you will find that they are not pine but ramin, a light-coloured hardwood. To find softwood mouldings you have to go to a joinery firm, such as Magnet Southerns, which has branches all over the country (look in the Yellow Pages), or get a carpenter to make a length to match. I improvised a moulding for a cupboard by cutting down an old piece of door architrave (figure 15) and this had the advantage of being made of old wood, so the colour matched. New mouldings can be stained to blend with the old by the procedure I have described on page 44, but remember to do your testing on the inside of the wood.

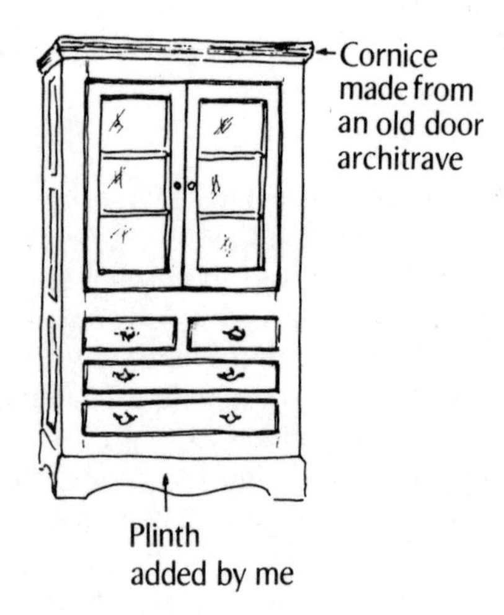

Fig 15

KNOBS BROKEN OR MISSING

The easiest solution is to remove all the knobs and replace them with reproduction knobs or brass handles. Many hardware stores stock them, or for a greater variety send for a catalogue from a specialist shop (several are listed on page 95). If you prefer the look of the old knobs, take one to a pine dealer to see if he has any that have been discarded in favour of brass fittings. If this fails, you can have one turned by a cabinet maker, though this will be more expensive.

MISSING FEET

Victorian bun feet (figure 16) can sometimes be supplied by a pine dealer because these are often replaced by a Georgian-style plinth. You may decide to have a plinth made instead of replacing the foot, or make one yourself. The method is described on page 74.

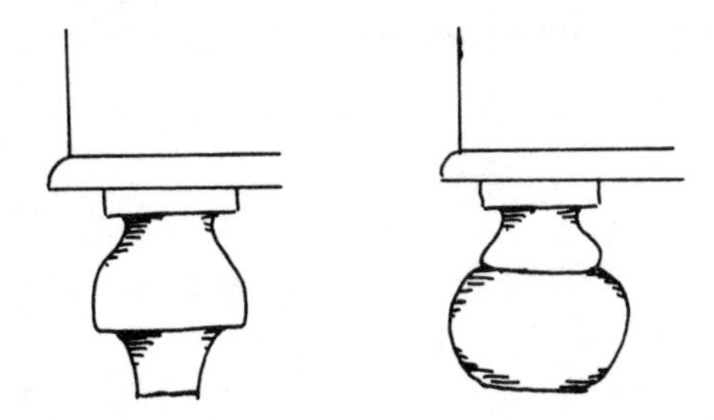

Fig 16

TARNISHED BRASS

Old brass handles and knobs are usually found in a dark brown opaque condition. This may be nothing but tarnish, but in case there is a layer of varnish, it is sensible to immerse them right away in paint stripper. This will remove any old coatings, and they can then be polished with a proprietary brass polish. If you still meet resistance, try dipping a cloth first in vinegar then in salt, and rubbing it over the brass. The combination of the acid in the vinegar and the bite of the salt works wonders. I use 00 steel wool as a last resort because it can scratch the surface of the brass. Prestige make a slightly abrasive Copper Cleaner in powder form which is excellent for cleaning brass and all metals, though you still need an application of ordinary brass polish to get a real glow.

You can lacquer your brass handles and knobs to keep them bright, but I prefer them left in their natural state.

6 · Adaptations

There are certain pieces of furniture which were always produced in large quantities – washstands, wardrobes, cupboards – and if you look at them with an open mind, often another use will suggest itself. Take, for example, the ubiquitous washstand.

Washstands

A lot of these were made, in a variety of styles, in the days before plumbing extended right through the house. Not many people can spare the space in a bedroom for what is now a purely decorative piece of furniture, but as dressing tables they can have a new and useful life. My favourite washstands are the ones with a round hole cut in the top for a basin, particularly if I can find a basin to fit. There is plenty of room around the edges of the hole for bottles and other dressing table paraphernalia.

Small washstands make good bedside tables. The narrow ones with square tops are rather early and not easy to find, but they are perfect for this. They usually have a little shelf halfway down, sometimes with a shallow drawer underneath. If the top has a basin hole cut in it and you want to put a lamp on it, you might like to place a sheet of glass over the whole top.

Many washstands make excellent desks. Some have high edges around three sides, which have a most satisfactory confining effect. If you meet a hole in this top, you will have to cover

Fig 17

it with a strong blotter! Be sure to check that your washstand/desk will accommodate a chair and knees under the working surface, and that it is a good height for writing. Sometimes there is a lower shelf, and you may have to cut this away into a concave shape (figure 17).

In the United States, the sort of washstand that has a narrow central cupboard (figure 18) is sometimes converted to a bathroom sink unit. The sink itself is fitted into the top, and the plumbing concealed in the cupboard below.

Fig 18

Washstands can be used as side tables, in any room in the house, but there are some with three legs, or with two heavy pedestals, which seem to look particularly good as hall tables.

Wardrobes

You can still use these as wardrobes, though some are rather shallow, with pegs inside for clothes to be hung on, rather than a rail for coat hangers. If you want to convert them, you may only have enough depth for a rail that goes from front to back. In my kitchen, I have a small wardrobe that I use as a broom cupboard, and I can't imagine a better one. The door is narrower than the cupboard, making little alcoves inside to right and left, so I built some shallow shelves on one side to take cleaning supplies. There were already several coat hooks which I use for hanging brooms and mops, and the vacuum cleaner stands on the floor. Underneath is a drawer, where I keep my rags and dusters (figure 19).

Wardrobes are often quite cheap, and it may be worth buying

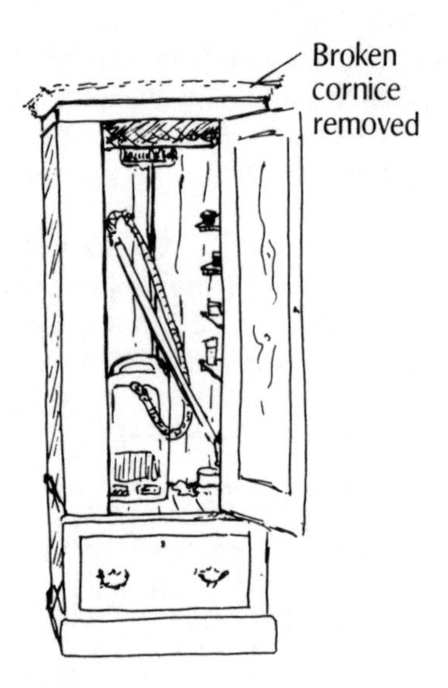

Fig 19

one just for the wood, which can be made into sets of shelves, kitchen cupboards, or anything else not readily available. You could also make one into a long low seat, by cutting the top off above the drawer, and laying one of the sides on top of the drawer section.

Cupboards

These turn up in every conceivable shape and size, and given time, you could furnish a whole kitchen with appropriately sized cupboards. For a couple of years I carried around the measurements of my metal sink unit, hoping for a pine one to replace it. At last I found one in a sale. I got it very cheaply for the good reasons that the bottom was damaged by woodworm, and the whole was covered in the brown paint which leaves a red stain behind it. It was quite a job to strip. The paint came off easily, but I didn't then know any of the techniques for removing the red stain (see p. 52), and so I tried to sand it off. This worked on the flat surfaces, but not on the mouldings and crevices. On the other hand, the cupboard had nice panelled doors, and fitted exactly under the stainless steel sink. I slipped the old unit out and the new in, without disturbing any of the plumbing.

'Slipped' gives a rather false impression – I had to destroy the old unit, and remove back, top and floor from the new! Recently I decided to have another go at the colour, which still bothered me. I used white spirit to strip off my polish and wax finish, gave the cupboard a coat of medium oak stain, and polyurethaned it. The darker stain now conceals the traces of red.

Many of us are torn between the desire for a comfortable old-fashioned kitchen, and the practical needs of a family. The image of the old cottage kitchen with its big wooden table, and armchair drawn up near a glowing range, has led us to reintroduce the pine dressers and tables once rejected by the Formica brigade. There is good reason for this reversal, because most people nowadays spend a lot of time in their kitchens and prefer a living room atmosphere – not that of a laboratory or hospital. But today's cook still needs somewhere to work and keep her equipment, and this has led to the adaptation of old cupboards to conceal modern fixtures. Manufacturers, catching on to this idea of blending old and new, are producing modern kitchen units with wooden doors, polished, painted or antiqued, along with a variety of tiled and wooden work surfaces, as an alternative to Formica. Some manufacturers will also supply wooden doors on their own, to fit existing units in your kitchen. If these new doors have to blend with old pine furniture, ask the supplier to leave them bare, because the colour of a modern finish will not do. Some manufacturers have an alternative antique pine finish, which may be satisfactory; otherwise you will have to stain them yourself (see pages 44 and 92).

If you are starting from scratch, you may be able to find a selection of old doors, and have a carpenter build suitable cupboards to fit them and fill the available space. I even know someone who used huge old chopping boards from an army surplus store to make the doors and work tops for his new kitchen.

Kitchens are not the only rooms in the house to need storage space, and in many cases you can improvise with semi-derelict pieces of furniture. Remove ugly doors from a cupboard, for instance, and use the frame as a bookcase. Good doors can be salvaged from a sagging frame and fitted to a new cupboard, or adapted to suit an alcove. Almost any size and shape of cupboard can be put to good use in a child's room. I adapted a shallow cupboard for my daughter's clothes, putting in two shelves at the top and a rail in the lower half for dresses. Unfortunately I forgot how much a child can grow in a year, so the dresses are now dragging on the cupboard floor. In the same bedroom is a dolls house I made out of another cupboard (figure 20). In fact I have made two, and a small shallow cupboard is a very good beginning for a dolls house, particularly if you have no carpentry skills. The only tricky bit is cutting holes for the windows and door, for which you need a portable jigsaw.

Fig 20

Tables

The reprinted volume of *Heal's Catalogues of 1853–1934* shows that countless numbers of 'deal-topped' tables were made in the 30s and 40s. There are pictures of all the familiar styles – straight-legged 'Georgian' ones, and bulbous 'Victorian' ones, many of which must now be on the market as antiques. Small, unexceptional pine tables are easily found and most adaptable. The legs can be cut down slightly to make a wonderful childrens' desk, or cut down further for a generous coffee table.

When it comes to kitchen or dining tables of a good generous size, the competition becomes stiff. Dealers make new tops for old bases, new bases for old tops, and whole new tables out of old wood. Often turned legs are left painted, in the tradition of the 'scrubbed' kitchen table – dark legs, pale top. If you are looking for a really big table, especially a round one, you will have to join the queue. You may be lucky and find an old base, in which case someone can make you a new top, preferably out of old wood (an old wardrobe?). Perhaps you are more interested in size than looks, and if so, you might use an ordinary trestle base and have a long top made. If, in despair, you are reduced to buying a brand new table – and there are many pine ones available – remove the plastic finish and apply a stain to tone down the raw colour of the wood (p. 92).

Chairs

You can make up a set of chairs by collecting them singly, and then altering the colour of any that do not match. The search will be easier if you stick to the most common type of plain wooden chair: the Windsor. You are probably familiar with the classic bow-backed and wheel-backed Windsors, and there is another common one called a 'lath-back' or 'slat-back', which has a wide back rail into which are fixed long vertical laths, shaped to the contours of the body. My own favourite of the Windsors is the Scroll-back, so called because the uprights of the back finish in a scroll, or backwards curve at the top. These are like the uprights on a Regency dining or side chair, and perhaps because of this style-link, they seem to be at home in any room in the house.

Between the uprights there are two bars, of which the lower one is sometimes turned, sometimes flat (figure 21.)

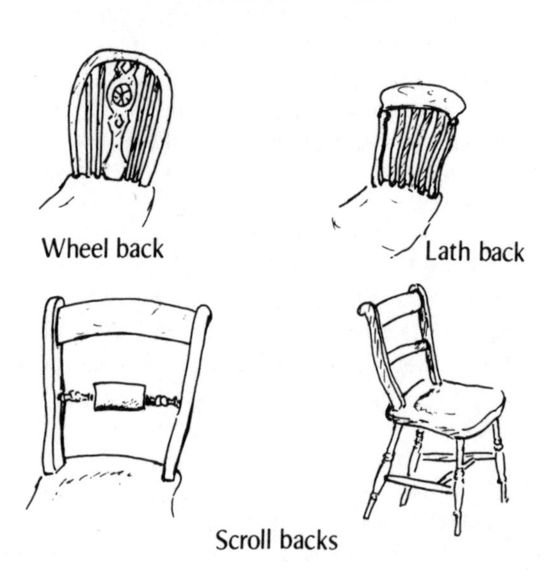

Fig 21

All of these chairs were produced in huge quantities in the last century, and some are still made today. They were sturdily built, and many have survived in good solid condition, despite being pushed around kitchens, barber shops, tea shops, and the like, for any number of years. The tremendous advantage of this mass production is the selection it provides for anyone trying to collect a set of chairs. Carvers, the ones with arms, also exist, though they are in demand singly as side chairs, and therefore harder to find.

The matching of colour and finish is the most tricky part of making up a set of chairs. Some are painted, some have been stripped to a hopeless grey colour, and others have their original nut-brown finish. You can keep looking, or buy odd ones and make them match (p. 43). If you want a lighter style of chair, you can collect balloon backs (figure 22), which have long

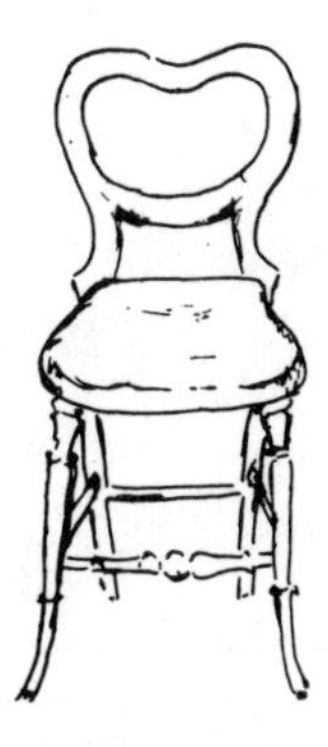

Balloon back

Fig 22

tapered legs, and upholstered or caned seats. These chairs are often a bit frail for everyday use, but they look well in bedrooms.

Mirrors

Mirrors are not difficult to find, but they may be expensive, because everyone wants them. A bevelled edge to the glass is a good indication that a mirror is in its original frame. The conversion of a dressing table into the more saleable desk, often yields three mirrors: a large central one, and two narrow side ones, all with marks on the sides of the frames from the old fittings. The two thin ones make good hall mirrors, side by side, and the central one is large enough to be useful anywhere.

You can improvise a mirror by putting new mirror glass into an old picture frame. If you want a pine one, look for a veneered frame. If some of the veneer is missing, which often happens, such a frame can be had quite cheaply. Strip off the rest of the veneer by immersing it overnight in a bathtub of water; the old glues dissolve very readily. Another less traditional use for an old picture frame is as the front of a shallow display box. You make – or have made – a simple box with shelves to fit behind the frame. If you use thin plywood, it can be glued into the rebate of the frame – the recess at the back for the glass. Four to six inches is a good depth for the box, and you can paint or line the inside, and use it to display china, miniature furniture or anything else.

Boxes

One very useful piece of furniture is The Box. Polished and waxed and sold as mule chests, they are expensive, but they can be found unstripped in junk shops. I stripped a smallish one with handles on the sides, which had once been a document box, and made it into a low bedside table (p. 88). It could equally well have been lined and used as a sewing box. Big blanket boxes make excellent coffee tables, and they can do double duty by storing board games. They look nice standing at the end of a bed, storing blankets as they originally did, or they can hold all the dressing-up clothes. You could make a big cushion for the top and use one as a window seat, or even upholster the whole of the top. Upholstered, it becomes an ottoman, and many blanket boxes turn up in this form.

Old trunks can often be used for the same purposes, though those with domed lids have obvious disadvantages. Trunks which are covered in leather paper are often very rough underneath, and they will need a lot of sanding before they are usable.

Dressers

Pine dressers have been sought after for years, and are always expensive. If you want to improvise one, buy an old cupboard of a suitable shape, and then look for a set of shelves which can hang on the wall above it. Obviously the shelves must be nearly the same width as the cupboard, and suitable in style and shape. You can have the shelves made, if you can't find any to fit, and even this expense will not bring it up to dresser price.

7 · Improvements and Decorative Painting

Perhaps you are now staring in despair at the results of your stripping. The dressing table that you took to be pine, has turned out to be a mysterious grey-brown wood, with no noticeable grain. The handles, cleaned of paint, are clearly of some base metal, and there is a large black mark on the table top. Don't give up. This may not be the perfect piece you wanted to match the rest of your bedroom furniture, but it is surprising how many improvements can be effected.

First take care of any structural defects like sticking drawers, and remove the black mark with oxalic acid (p. 55).

Handles and Knobs

Scrap the metal handles and get some new ones. Most hardware stores now carry a basic range of brass fittings, or write for a catalogue to J.D. Beardmore (3–5 Percy St, London W1P 0EJ) for a wide selection of everything brass. Beardmores have an amazing range of fittings. I was able to replace the rusty iron drop handles on my kitchen table with identical brass ones – even the screw holes were in the same place. When choosing your replacement handles, take along one of the old ones, so that you can make sure that the new back plates will cover the holes from the old.

If you are dissatisfied with the 'brassy' look of your new handles, soak them in paint stripper to remove the lacquered finish. Then you can either wait for time to tarnish and darken them or, for a more drastic solution, put them in a hot oven for a few hours. This sounds rather extreme, but I know it works, because I have just finished cleaning some brass candlesticks that inadvertently had this treatment. A friend had put them in a warm oven to remove the congealed candle wax (a few moments under the hot tap would have done the job better), forgotten about them, and let them cook with the Sunday roast. I have myself put new brass hinges, wrapped in aluminium foil, into the ashes at the base of a wood fire, and an evening of this also turns them a good colour.

Before putting the new brass handles onto your piece of furniture, you must tackle any staining, painting or structural changes that need doing. I will d eal with the structural ones first.

Plinths

Sometimes you find yourself with a piece of furniture that is basically attractive, but with features that don't suit you or your room. Take, for example, a Victorian chest of drawers. It may be a good shape, with well-grained wood, but its knobs and bun feet look out of place with the rest of your furniture (figure 23).

Fig 23

Whether one should always keep original features is largely a matter of taste. I have grown fond of these knobs and feet, but many dealers remove them in favour of brass Georgian-style handles and a shaped plinth. You can do this too. The handle part is easy (see above), but the plinth will involve you in some carpentry. You need three strips of wood – the front and two sides – each with an arch cut out to form bracket feet. This arch can be plain or complicated (figure 24), and to cut it you need a jigsaw, or a fretsaw, or a friend with one of these. The wood should be ¾ inch thick, with the top edge rounded. Ideally you should mitre the corners where the sides meet the front, and glue blocks behind (figures 25 and 26), to support the weight of the chest of drawers, but for a quick cosmetic effect, you can make the plinth in the following way: remove any bottom mouldings, and screw or nail the new shaped base directly to the front and sides of the chest, leaving the feet in place to support its weight. The

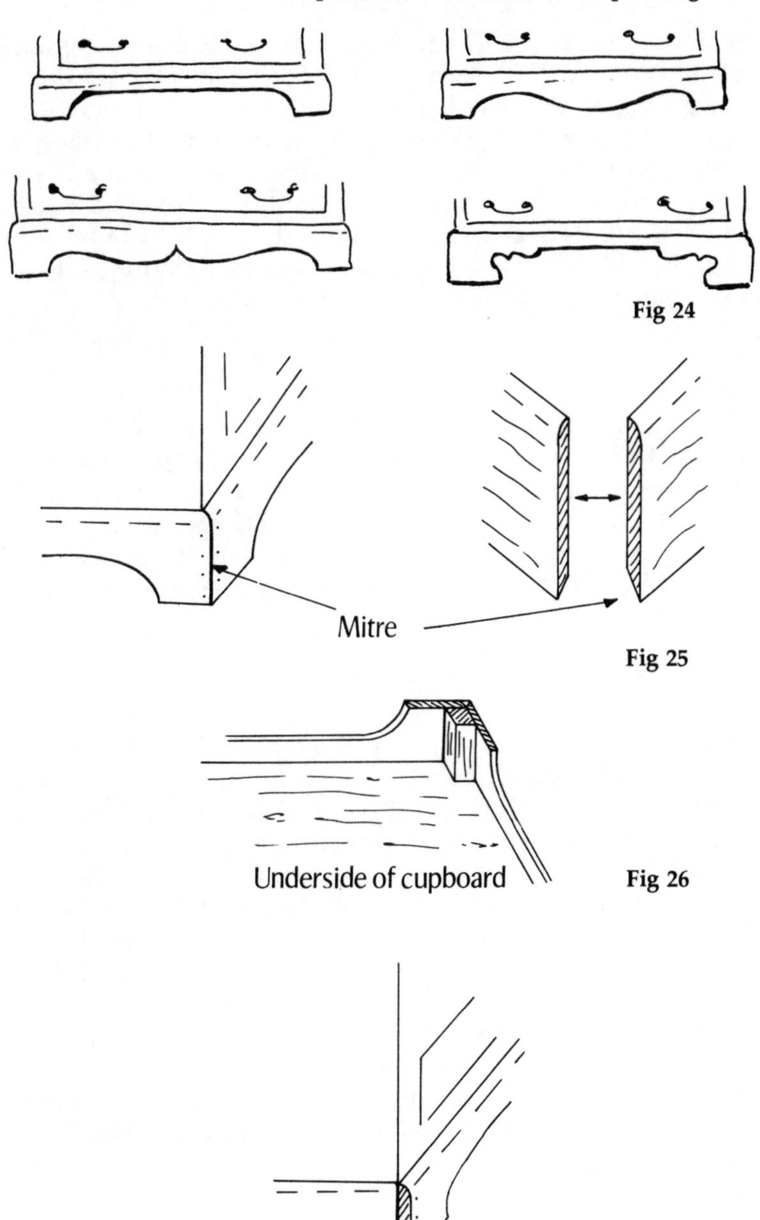

Fig 24

Fig 25

Fig 26

Fig 27

front piece needs to be long enough to cover the ends of the side pieces (figure 27). This sort of cobbled job will not stand up to being dragged about too much.

There are some old chests of drawers or cupboards that already have a plinth, but one that is completely straight – just a board around the bottom. These look very heavy, and are much improved by having a shape cut out of the plinth, as I have just described. With a hand-held power jigsaw, the cutting can be done without removing the plinth from the chest.

Tiles

Some washstands have truly hideous tiles in livid colours along the back, and it is a simple matter to replace them. They are usually held in place by a piece of wood screwed to the back of the frame. You can keep your eyes open for antique replacement tiles, which are easily found if you only need a few, or you can buy new ones which are in keeping with the style of the washstand. Don't forget to carry the measurements of the old tiles with you.

Plywood

Plywood turns up everywhere – in panels, in old repairs, or even, if you are very unlucky, as the top or sides of a piece of furniture. This ply is prone to warping, and it provides a happy home for woodworm. On the other hand, the presence of plywood in a piece of furniture brings the price down dramatically, and there are many ways of camouflaging it.

Easiest of all is to accept it, and stain it in a slightly warmer tone than the rest of the wood. This counteracts its usual greyish cast. At the other extreme, you can remove the plywood altogether and replace it with solid wood. For most people, this means handing over to a carpenter. To get a panel out of a cupboard door, for instance, the whole frame of the door has to be dismantled, first knocking out the pegs that hold it together. A new panel is then cut and bevelled, and the frame reassembled and glued, leaving the panel 'floating' to allow for expansion and contraction of the wood. A simpler, but even more expensive replacement is a panel of brass mesh. Beardmores sell all kinds, and it does give a nice Regency Bookcase look, which would suit a formal piece. You may be able to install it yourself, if the frame of your door has a 'rebate', which is a recessed edge behind the moulding (figure 28), such as you find in picture frames. If so, first remove the moulding, then cut round the plywood with a jigsaw or fretsaw, close to the edge of the frame. Glue the moulding back in place, and then staple the brass mesh to the back of the moulding with a staple gun (or use tacks).

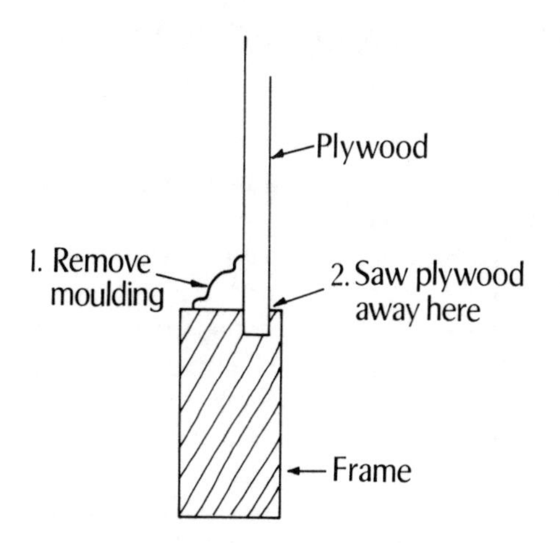

Fig 28

The same method can be used to replace plywood with a panel of pre-woven cane. This looks exactly like a cane seat, but is prefabricated, and can be cut to any size. Order it from Berry's Craft Supplies, 10 Hill Rd., Theydon Bois, Epping, Essex. Tel: 037 881 3532.

A simple solution to the plywood panel is to cover it. If the object is going in a bedroom, or somewhere not too formal, you can use paper or fabric. You can of course use wallpaper, but the paper I like best with wood is ordinary brown wrapping paper – the sort with fine, almost imperceptible lines on it. It is called 'kraft' paper, and most stationers sell it in rolls. The colour can vary quite a lot, from salmon to warm to dark brown. Fix the paper to the panels, dull side out, with wallpaper paste. This works perfectly, and indeed I have wallpapered a whole room with kraft paper.

Fabric can also be applied to wood with wallpaper paste, or

better still, with starch, and in either case, seal the wood first with a coat of shellac (or French polish). Mix powdered starch with water to the consistency of a medium white sauce, and sponge it onto the back of the fabric, then press in place. Firm fabrics like chintz and cotton are easier to handle when pasted. You can cover a whole piece of furniture with fabric and even paste it onto the wall behind – the starch makes the fabric soil-resistant.

COLOURED STAINS, PAINT, AND ANTIQUE FINISHES

Coloured stains

General instructions for finishing stripped pine are given in Chapter 4, but you may need a more dramatic treatment for a really unsatisfactory piece of furniture. Unattractive wood benefits greatly from staining, so first try out one or two of the ordinary wood stains on an inconspicuous part. Sometimes a coat of medium oak is enough to warm up a dull wood and give it character. If you are dissatisfied with this, you might like to use a bright colour, like green or blue. There are coloured varnishes on the market which look marvellous when they are first applied, but beware! Because the colour is carried in the varnish coat, and does not sink into the wood like a stain, it also comes off with the varnish. Every scratch and knock reveals bare, uncoloured wood. There are coloured wood dyes made by Dygon or Furniglas (if you can find them), or you can obtain, from Fiddes of Cardiff, powdered stains which are soluble either in water or in methylated spirits. You can also improvise, which is what I do. Here is my method:

Pour some of the lightest wood dye you can find (light oak will do) into a bowl, enough for the whole piece of furniture. Then stir in a good squirt of Universal Stainer in the colour you desire. These stainers are used for tinting paint, and are available in tubes from most decorating or Do-It-Yourself shops. When you have the colour you like, simply apply it, as usual (p. 45) to the piece of furniture. Finish off with a coat of polyurethane or whatever else you like (Chapter 4). One advantage of this method is that the brownish cast of the wood dye tones down the primary colours of the stainers.

It is also possible to use Dylon ordinary fabric dyes, applying a concentrated solution with a rag. The disadvantage of water-soluble dyes is that they raise the grain of the wood. It will have to be sanded again when dry.

When your dressing table has had its coats of stain, polish, and wax, put on the new handles, and you should be well pleased with the result. If not, put it in an auction and start again, or use:

Paint

It may seem strange to talk about painting furniture in a book about stripping, but sometimes you find a piece which is just not redeemable with stains, additions, or new brass fittings. Paint is the ultimate camouflage – to cover offending areas of plywood, or as a coat for an entire piece of furniture. Perhaps your piece is made up of three different, unblending woods, or it may be a dull, heavy shape, unrelieved by any good features. Rather than painting it with ordinary gloss paint, there are a variety of decorative finishes which can transform an ordinary object into one that blends with any period of furniture.

All of these finishes start with a good base coat of ordinary paint: emulsion (latex), eggshell or undercoat can be used. I prefer the oil-based paints because they are less porous than emulsion, making it easier to apply a glaze smoothly. Colour is the most important factor. In general, the colours that were used on the old painted pine furniture look best – soft blues and blue-greens, pale brick red, light brown, maize yellow etc. I buy a standard eggshell paint in the colour nearest to the one I want, and then tint it to my final shade with Universal Stainers or artists' oils. In the United States, excellent paints are available in standard ranges with names like 'Mayflower Red' and 'Decatur Buff', which reproduce the old Colonial and Federal colours. The actual colours used in the eighteenth century would have been much more vivid, but our taste has been conditioned by looking at the mellowed paint on old houses and furniture.

Before you set to work, remove any hardware, and make sure that your surface is sound and smooth. Next apply a coat of shellac (or French polish) to seal the wood and give a good base, or use primer and undercoat. Rub down the shellac or undercoat with 00 wire wool to get rid of imperfections, and then apply your top coat of paint – or two coats if you find you need them. Now you are ready for the decoration, and there are several options: you can apply a stencilled design, lining, an antique glaze, or all three of these. The glaze is the simplest, so I will describe that first. It is a transparent, slightly shiny coat, tinted with a small amount of pigment. When applied to a painted surface and then partially rubbed off, a residue of colour remains in the grain and in crevices, giving a time-worn effect.

Antique glaze

You need the following supplies:

- A small tin of 'transparent oil glaze' or clear 'scumble glaze', obtainable from specialist paint shops (look in the Yellow Pages).
- Artists' oil paint (see below for colours) or Universal Stainers
- Turpentine or white spirit
- A paint brush, two inches wide or more
- Rags or paper towels
- Clear varnish, if protection is needed

Here is how to mix and apply the glaze:

1 You need to tint the glaze, and you can use any colour that looks good over the base coat. If you just want a look of aging, go for the browns – raw umber, burnt umber – or black. In a bowl or jar put a blob of the tinting colour you have chosen, and add a little white spirit to dissolve it. Pour in the glaze and stir it well to disperse the colour. Then you must thin the glaze with white spirit to a runny consistency, using the proportions of one part of glaze to one of white spirit to start with, and adding more solvent if it still seems thick. It should be as runny as milk.

2 Dip your brush in the glaze and paint it freely over one section of your piece of furniture – a door, a whole side, or the top. Don't be dismayed by runs and drips. Leave it for a few seconds, then wipe most of it off with the rags or paper towels. The trick is to leave more of the glaze in corners and crevices, where time would have gathered dirt. In the centre of panels and

along exposed edges, rub most of the glaze off. If you feel that your attempts look blotchy, just rub off *all* the glaze lightly. Enough will remain in the grain to give a subtle effect.

3 Let the glaze dry, then apply a coat of varnish if the piece will get a lot of wear or need washing. If this makes the surface too glossy, rub it down with 00 or 000 steel wool.

I keep a small tin of glaze tinted with burnt umber, and I use it as an all-purpose final coat for painted sections of otherwise plain wood furniture. It is very effective, for instance, over green or blue paint, inside a cupboard or on the back wall of a dresser. The glaze tones down the brightness of modern paints and helps them blend in with mellow old wood.

If you feel rather more ambitious, you can try some other decorative treatments. One that is a good deal easier than it looks is 'lining' (also called striping).

Lining

This process consists of a fine line, about an eighth of an inch thick, drawn freehand around drawer fronts, down legs, inside panels, etc. It outlines and highlights any good features, and adds interest where there is none (figure 29). The only materials you need are:

- A small tin of satin (mid-sheen) or flat varnish
- A tube of Artists' oil paint in the colour desired (if in doubt, raw umber looks good over most backgrounds)
- White spirit
- A good quality artist's brush, size 3.

Those are the materials that I use, but you can also make the lining paint with Artists' acrylic or gouache paint thinned with a little water. This works well over a flat base coat, but I prefer the varnish mixture because it flows on smoothly, and gives a slightly transparent line that minimizes any wobble.

Lining usually goes on before the antique glaze. If you want to put it on afterwards, first seal the glaze with a coat of shellac or white French polish. This will allow you to rub off any mistakes without lifting the glaze.

Here is the method:

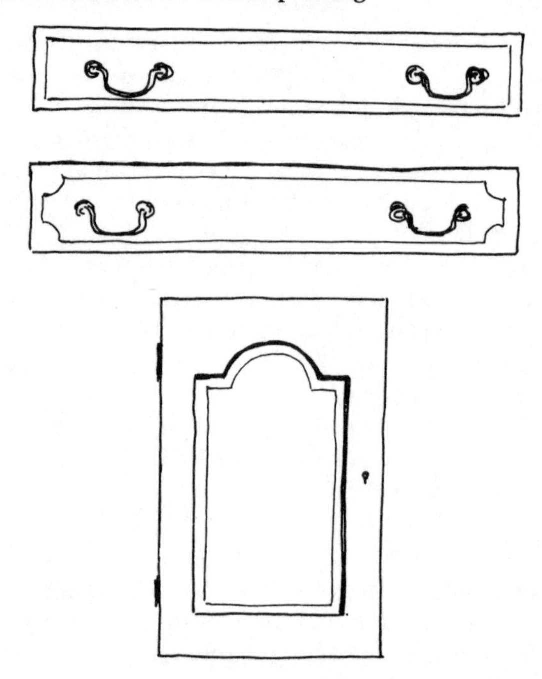

Fig 29

Lay your piece of furniture down, so that you are working on a flat surface. Dip the brush in the tinted varnish, and paint a line about half an inch in from an edge. Hold the brush halfway up between thumb and forefinger and draw it along, letting the other three fingers run loosely along the edge to steady your hand. Your first attempt may well be a disaster, but wipe it off with white spirit and try again. If you slip your hand along quickly you will find it easier to keep the line even – slowness leads to wobble and blobs. A certain amount of unevenness doesn't matter, and can add character to your work. Stand back from it and look at the general effect, saying to yourself as my aunt does, 'The man riding by wouldn't notice'.

On a long straight edge, I sometimes rule a faint pencil line as a guide, but it is important to paint *beside*, not over it, so that you can erase the pencil mark later. If you feel you really cannot draw the lines freehand, then isolate the areas you want painted with strips of masking tape, available from stationers and hardware stores. Press the inside edges of the tape down hard, so that the lining paint cannot seep under it. As a last resort, use felt tip pens and a straight edge (a long carpenter's ruler).

Stencils

Stencils are familiar to most of us from childhood days – those cut-out shapes of houses and cows that had to be filled in with paint. It is, in fact, a very old craft that has recently had a great upsurge in popularity, particularly in the United States. If you want to invent your own, special stencil paper is available in many art shops. Or you can buy them ready-made, some supplied in book-form. For stencilling you will need:

- Stencil paper, varnished card, or printed stencils
- A sharp craft knife
- Acrylic or any quick-drying paints
- A short fat brush or some bits of velvet

To make your own pattern, first draw a simple design, leaving strips of paper to tie one piece to another (figure 30), and then cut out the pieces with the craft knife. One tip: it is easier to cut curves if you hold the knife still and move the paper instead. Tape the finished stencil to the piece of furniture with masking tape, and dab paint sparingly through the holes with the brush or a piece of velvet. The brush can be a shaving brush, or a round fat child's brush with the bristles cut short. Velvet gives a soft,

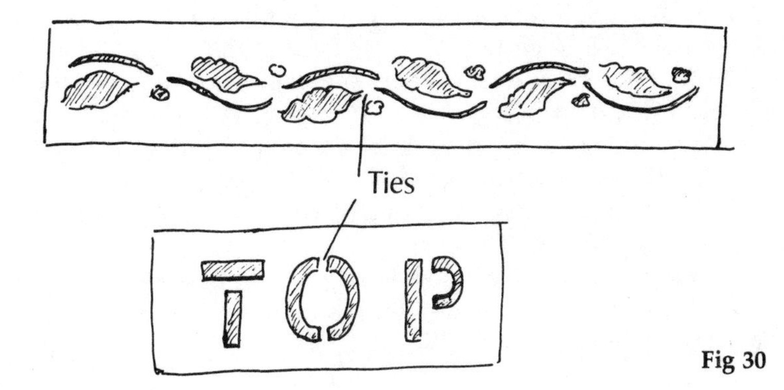

Fig 30

shaded effect that is very attractive. If using a brush, don't overload the bristles with paint, or it may creep under the edges of the stencil.

For borders or large patterns, the stencil will have to be moved and reused, and you must wait till the paint has dried or it will smudge. To speed things up, you might like to make several copies of any pattern that repeats.

The antique glaze that I have already described makes a good final coat over the finished stencil, toning down the colours and helping them to blend together.

Antique painted pine effect

This is a phoney way of achieving the look of old painted furniture which has worn slightly, revealing patches of bare wood.

The materials you need are:

- A bottle of button polish (brown tinted French polish)
- A tin of paint in a dark antique colour like slate blue or blue-green (or tint your own as on p. 79)
- Rags or paper towels
- Antique glaze (p. 80)
- Teak stain (if your wood is very pale)

The method is as follows:

1 Apply a coat of Blackfriars' Teak stain if needed, otherwise proceed to next step.

2 Rub on two coats of button polish with a cloth, letting each one dry (1 to 3 hours).

3 Paint on one coat of your chosen paint, and before it dries:

4 Rub it off in places where it would get the most wear – around handles, along the edges of doors and drawers, etc.

5 Let the rest of the paint dry.

6 Finish with a coat of antique glaze.

If you get to the rubbing off stage and don't like the look, you can always paint the whole thing and adopt one of the other decorative finishes.

All the painted finishes I have described can be improved by a few final touches. Most will benefit from a good rub down with steel wool and wax, which will soften the whole effect. Review the handle situation: do the wooden knobs now look too heavy? If so, replace them with brass knobs or drop handles. I allow myself this sort of extravagant extra as a reward for doing all the stripping and painting myself.

The transformation of a piece of furniture that seemed beyond rescue, into one fit for any room in the house, is incredibly satisfying. I realise that some of the techniques are daunting to read about, but none of them is at all difficult once you start. They require no artistic talent except in choosing the basic paint colour, and you can always settle for something safe, like grey or cream. Even an untidy worker will find that an overall coat of antique glaze hides most faults and makes them seem the result of time, not carelessness – remember the man riding by!

8 · Case histories

In this chapter I shall first describe various trials I have made with new products on the market which claim to strip ten or more coats in one go. The second half of the chapter is taken up with some of my own attempts at stripping and refinishing furniture, using conventional methods.

NEW PRODUCTS

Peel-Away

Peel-Away, which contains caustic soda, has to be mixed with water in its tub, and in my case came out like thick cream. I applied it to an old door on which at least four layers of paint were visible through the chips. There is a plastic spatula provided, with which you spread the paste quite thickly. You then wet a special 'blanket' (also provided, but in an awkward long strip), and press it onto the pasted surface, where it sticks. The leaflet tells you to put down plenty of newspapers or a plastic sheet, but I was a bit casual about this, only to find that the blanket dripped dissolved paint onto the floor. I definitely recommend a piece of polythene sheeting under the newspaper, especially as the subsequent stages become progressively messier. After two hours you are supposed to peel the blanket slowly off, helping the paint along with the spatula so that it comes off on the blanket, which it *mostly* does. The remaining bits were a problem, with the choice of reapplying the paste and blanket, or resorting to a scraper. There would probably have been no bits remaining if I had spread the paste to an even thickness, but this is remarkably hard to do over a wide area. I tried scrubbing and rinsing, as the leaflet suggests, but my last few pieces of paint remained undissolved.

Verdict: quite a bit of mess of the familiar caustic soda variety, with brown sludge dripping onto the floor, and the risk of crystallization on same, if not properly neutralised. Also expensive, though all tools and rubber gloves are provided. Cleaning the re-usable blanket was almost the worst part of the whole business, because it was encrusted with hard old paint and varnish that had to be scraped off.

I tried it out on a stone fireplace, where Ronstrip cannot be used. I had once stripped another one by scraping and stabbing with shavehooks, because I had been warned that paint stripper would discolour the stone, but it had taken me days of work. The Peel-Away did seem worthwhile here, because it pulled the paint right out of the crevices – even a black bituminous layer. It would also be very useful on delicate and intricate plaster mouldings or cornices. Not appropriate, in my opinion, for stripping large surfaces like doors, because of the cost and the mess. The caustic content darkens hardwoods, which further limits its use.

Ronstrip

This has many of the built-in problems of Peel-Away. It is messy and expensive, and has the additional drawback of being unsuitable for stone and plaster.

I used the ready-mixed variety on another bit of the same door. It was a bit stiffer than toothpaste, and again I found it hard to follow the instructions about applying a thick even coat. The manufacturers recommend covering it with plastic to stop it drying out, so I used the thin foodwrap sold on rolls for wrapping sandwiches. It is inexpensive and stuck beautifully to the paste. A penetrating time of up to ten hours is recommended, which meant that I applied it mid-morning when my energy is always highest, and it was ready to come off between six and eight in the evening, when I was trying to cook supper and had lost all interest in stripping. As a result, I left the paste till the next morning, but the plastic wrap had kept it moist, and most of it scraped off quite readily. Once again, however, my uneven application meant that some patches remained unstripped. I reapplied some of the scraped-off paste, covered it again, and after another few hours they came off.

Verdict: another messy process, with dissolved paint dripping onto the floor and lots of scraping and rinsing at the end. I also tried the Ronstrip Peel-off version which comes in powder form, and is more economical. This wouldn't peel off for me, but it scraped off quite well like the paste variety. Like caustic soda,

Ronstrip darkens hardwoods, and unless you rinse it off very thoroughly, it leaves a grubby deposit on the surface from the dissolved paints. All in all, not much improvement that I could see on ordinary chemical strippers, unless you really do have ten layers to remove.

Nitromors' Break-thru

Break-thru comes in a transparent plastic pot, and is an appealing green gel. It smells like a chemical paint stripper, and contains no caustic, so it can be used on hardwoods. As with the previous two products, you had to spread on a thick layer and leave it, this time uncovered. I tried it on a wooden stool with two visible layers of paint. Absolutely nothing happened, except that the Break-thru hardened into an immovable skin. I wrote to the manufacturers explaining my problem and asking for another tub. First a tin of ordinary Nitromors chemical stripper arrived through the post, and then a letter saying that they were having trouble with the Break-Thru containers, and that the active solvents had evaporated from mine before I could use it. Presumably when they sort out this problem the stuff will work, but it is still very expensive. They illustrate it being used on a Grandfather clock, with the layers coming away in one coat, and as there is no wetting involved, it would be worth using on a valuable antique that had inadvertently been painted.

Although each of these new products has its uses, the easiest and cheapest stripper for pine furniture is still caustic soda, and the next section will include some of my experiences while using it.

CONVENTIONAL STRIPPING

Document box, using chemical paint stripper

I bought this wooden document box quite cheaply in a junk shop, because I noticed that it had nice brass carrying handles (by this I mean the sort that will only lift up halfway, till they are horizontal). It was covered in thick dark varnish.

I spread newspapers over the kitchen floor, selected an old gummy paintbrush that needed softening, put on my kitchen rubber gloves, and set to. I decided not to remove the brass handles at the sides.

Using Blackfriars paint stripper, which is a gel, I tipped a small amount of stripper onto one side of the box, and spread it with the brush. I left it a few moments, and then dabbed some more over the top. When I could see that the whole surface was bubbling up, I scraped it off with a metal scraper. A second coat was scrubbed off with 0 grade steel wool. It became apparent that there was some brown stain that was resisting the stripper, so I scrubbed harder with the steel wool, and more came off. The colour was now a warm goldy-brown, and I decided that it would do. I stripped the rest of the box in the same way, turning it over so that I was always working on a flat surface, and leaving the top till last. About halfway through, I made two discoveries: one, my kitchen gloves were ruined (should have used old ones), and two, I was greatly hampered by the handles, which I had left on out of laziness. I took them off and work progressed much faster.

Because I had used a chemical stripper and no water, the box was dry and ready for finishing. The job so far had taken me under an hour. I finished the box with French polish and wax (p. 46) and cleaned the handles with salt and vinegar (p. 63). When they were polished and replaced on the box, it retired upstairs to become a small bedside table.

Beech stool — cold caustic bath

This square-legged stool, with an S-shaped carrying hole in the seat, was still covered in a skin of green Break-Thru. I immersed it in my caustic bath, and because it was beech and likely to rough-up, I hurried the process by turning it over and scrubbing away at the bits that were sticking out, rather than leaving the whole thing to soak for a few hours. The Break-Thru was extremely difficult to break through, and the places where it was thinnest came off first. In retrospect, it would probably have been better to dissolve it with ordinary Nitromors.

In less than an hour, all the paint was off, even from the top which was elm, with a very rough, open grain. I hosed it down and let it dry for fifteen minutes, before dousing it with vinegar. If the wood is superficially dry, you can see where you have put the vinegar and avoid missing patches. As a final touch, I turned the stool upside down and poured some vinegar into the frame, so that it would seep into the joints.

The seat warped a bit, but it flattened out again as it dried. There were rough patches where the wood had gone fluffy, and the seat was very bad indeed, due to its previous open air life in an army surplus yard. To make sure there were no splinters in the seat, I first sanded it with a flapwheel (p. 42), which did a good job of eating down to solid wood, following the contours worn in the seat. Then with medium sandpaper, followed by fine, I smoothed down the rest of the stool. I decided to try out a new oil-based finish, and I have described it on page 94.

Nest of three tables — cold caustic bath

I put all three tables into the bath, hooking them inside each other, and weighing the whole down with a strategically placed brick. After two hours, I took them out one at a time and scrubbed them with a Scotchbrite scourer, while dribbling over water from a hose. The paint, which was a red imitation lacquer, came off in sheets, and the undercoat washed off easily. The tops had a

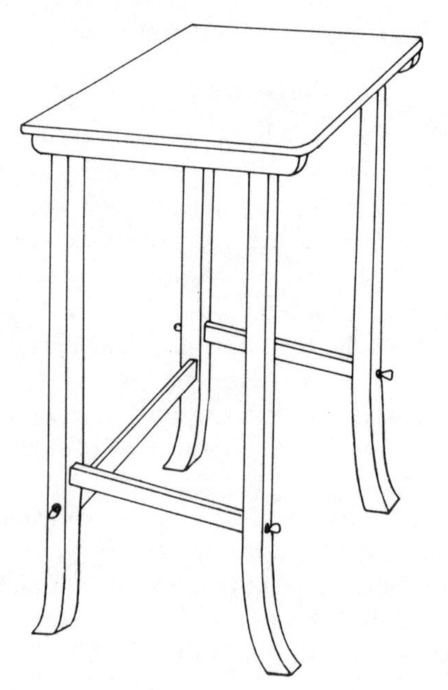

Fig 31

hideous imitation lacquer top complete with Chinese scenes, and the caustic only nibbled this away at the edges, revealing a layer of Chinese newspaper underneath.

After stripping what I could, I put the tables back in the bath, turned over so that the caustic could work on another section. A couple of hours later I got the same results on these bits, and the tables were now mostly down to the bare wood. The exceptions were some knobs which screwed into the legs (figure 31), the occasional patch on a stretcher, and most of the tops. This time I replaced them tops downward in the bath, and left them for an hour. Still hardly any effect on the black lacquer, so rather than over-wet the tables, I decided to strip any remaining patches with paint stripper.

As I had to leave them for the time being, I neutralised them carefully with vinegar. Although they are pine, small strips of wood have been glued onto the sides of the legs to make them curve out at the bottom. The joins are very obvious, so I shall have to repaint the tables. I plan to use a brick red, toned down with an antique glaze, and I may also stencil a small border round the top.

Old cupboard – hot caustic

This was actually a small wardrobe which I eventually converted into a broom cupboard (p. 66).

I stripped it with hot caustic over a drain at the side of the house. It had only one coat of red-brown paint which came off like a dream leaving, inevitably, the dreaded Red Stain. When I had removed all traces of the paint by scrubbing with steel wool, I tackled the stain. First I tried domestic bleach, which had little effect, then methylated spirits, which removed some, but still left an allover faint redness. My last resort was a hot solution of washing soda, made with boiling water. This I scrubbed in with grade 1 (coarse) steel wool, and after two applications, the surface came clean. There were still the faintest traces here and there, especially in crevices that were difficult to get at, but on the whole it was liveable with. After neutralising with vinegar, I left it to dry, and then gave it the lightweight finish of French polish and wax described on page 46.

FINISHING AND REFINISHING

In this section I will describe some cosmetic changes made to unsatisfactory pieces of furniture, and also a few alternatives to the finishes I have recommended in Chapter 4.

Badly stripped blanket box

This was a pine box, bought already stripped and waxed, which had obviously stayed too long in a caustic tank. The wood was dry looking, and bleached to an unattractive staring white colour. I had been using it as a dressing up box, so its original wax finish had had no replenishing coats, and in addition the top was stained by rain because it had stood by a window.

To restore it, I first had to remove all the wax, and this I did by scrubbing with steel wool and white spirit. When the box dried, it had lost its shine and also the watermarks, which were apparently superficial. I gave the whole box a light sanding, and then a coat of Colron's Light Oak stain, thinking it would be just the right colour. In fact it was a little pale and cold, so I added a second coat of Medium Oak. This is not a good practice, because the wood accepts very little of the second stain, and I would have been better off mixing the two stains in a jar in the first place.

I let the stain dry overnight, and then painted on a coat of button polish. This is a brown form of French polish, and I used it because I was still not satisfied with the depth of my stain. When it dried, I rubbed the surface with 000 steel wool dipped in wax, to dull the shine. And then added two more coats of wax, polished with a cloth to a satin sheen. The improvement over the old bleached colour is amazing.

New pine table

This was a small low table of modern varnished pine, which was a bright shiny yellow colour. I removed the varnish in my caustic soda tank. The stripping could have been done with a chemical paint stripper, but the caustic has a darkening and mellowing effect on the new wood.

When it was neutralised and dry, I rubbed the table down well with sandpaper to smooth the surface and soften the hard edges. I then made a half-and-half mixture of Blackfriars Teak and Medium Oak stains, and wiped this on. I gave the table two coats of polyurethane varnish, rubbed down with fine steel wool between, and dulled the final coat with 000 steel wool dipped in dark tan shoe polish. Shoe polish is just wax with colour in it, and is very handy for touch-ups. The table was now a much better colour, but the wood still looked newish; the passage of time will tone it down further, and add depth to the colour.

Scrubbed pine table top

Scrubbed pine is for people who love hard work – therefore this is the description of a friend's table. As was common in the nineteenth century, the legs and frame of this table are covered in dark brown varnish, but the top is completely bare of any finish, even wax. When it looks grubby, which is almost every day, she sprinkles some scouring powder, such as Ajax or Vim, all over the dry top of the table. Then with a scrubbing brush or Scotch-brite scourer and warm water, she scrubs the table, using the powder as a mild abrasive and bleach. After several rinsings to remove the accumulated sludge, the table is left to dry, when it has a smooth white surface . . . until people start using it again. This was the normal finish for a wooden kitchen table in the days when people had servants, and Heal's was still selling them in 1923. Sometimes you find a table like this made of pitch pine, where the harder sections of the grain actually stand up in ridges from the constant scrubbing.

Imitation scrubbed pine

This is really a painted surface, applied thinly to a wooden table top in an attempt to copy the smooth pale surface of scrubbed pine. You need to use an oil-based paint in an off-white colour, diluted by an equal amount of white spirit. Rub this mixture into the grain of the wood, then with a clean cloth, rub it off again, leaving a haze of creaminess, with the wood showing through. When the paint is completely dry, apply a coat of varnish to protect it.

Colron liquid wax

I decided to try this wax – available in light, medium and dark – because the manufacturers claimed that it would add colour to the wood, and I hoped it might be useful for toning down new finishes. The wax comes in a tin like the stains, with a small top opening. So far, every time I have gone to use it, my liquid wax has actually been a thick paste, and wedged in its tin. I find it will only soften near a source of direct heat, which is unnerving as the contents are inflammable.

I tried the light and the medium on the blanket box I had just refinished, but couldn't detect any colour change. You are forbidden to use a paste wax on top because it lifts the 'colour', and with so many limitations, I can't see much point in these waxes. I recommend you to stick to the paste ones, and use shoe polish if you want to add a little colour.

Colron wood reviver

Another new product from Colron, and a useful one if you want a completely natural finish. The reviver is based on linseed oil, which penetrates into the wood, and it can be waxed on top.

I applied two coats to a beech stool that I had just stripped (p. 89), and it darkened the wood to the colour of old oak. Because I had not expected such a dramatic colour change, I had filled one or two small nail holes with walnut plastic wood, and these now stood out as pale spots. Apart from that, it was a very attractive finish for hardwoods, especially with several coats of wax on top, and suitable for decorative pieces of furniture. Spills of water and spirits show up as pale marks, so the reviver is not suitable for heavy use. I do not recommend any oil finishes on pine because they will discolour the wood and attract dirt.

I hope by now that you are feeling encouraged to try stripping wood yourself. Don't wait for a clear weekend – start now. Because there are several stages in stripping, all requiring pauses for drying time, it is an occupation that can be fitted into the odd spare moments of everyday life. I have had a lot of fun from looking for bargains and stripping pine, and I hope you will too.

Useful addresses

Architectural Salvage (p. 9):

Architectural Heritage of Cheltenham, Bayshill Lodge, Montpellier, Cheltenham Glos. Tel: Cheltenham 26567

Walcot Reclamation, 108 Walcot St, Bath BA1 5BG. Tel: Bath 310182

Or write with request to Architectural Salvage Agency at The Architectural Press, 9 Queen Anne's Gate, London SW1. Tel: 01-222 4333

Brass Fittings (pp. 63 and 73):

J.D. Beardmore & Co Ltd, 3–5 Percy St, London W1. Tel: 01-636 1214

B. Lilly & Sons Ltd, Baltimore Rd, Birmingham B42 1JD. Tel: 021–357 1761

Rothley Brass, Merrivale St, Wolverhampton, W. Midlands. Tel: Wolverhampton 27532

Wood and Brass Fittings of all kinds (p. 63):

Woodfit Ltd, Whittle Low Mill, Chorley, Lancs, PR6 7HB. Tel: Chorley 7279521.

Wooden Knobs in various woods (p. 62):

Winther, Browne & Co Ltd, 119 Downhills Way, Tottenham, London N16 5BR. Tel: 01-889 0971

Wooden Mouldings (p. 62):

General Woodwork Supplies, 76–78 Stoke Newington High St, London N16 5BR. Tel: 01-254 6052

Magnet Southerns (check Yellow Pages for local branches) head office:

Magnet Joinery Ltd, Keighley, W. Yorkshire. Tel: Keighley 61133

W.H. Newson, 481–489 Battersea Park Rd, London SW11 4NH. Tel: 01-223 4411

Doors (p. 67):

Just Doors, Unit 2, Limborough Rd, Wantage, Oxon. Tel: Wantage 65850

Solarbo Fitments Ltd, PO Box 5, Commerce Way, Lancing, West Sussex BN15 8TF. Tel: Lancing 63451/7.

Pre-Woven Cane (p. 77):

Berry's Craft Supplies, 10 Hill Rd, Theydon Bois, Epping, Essex. Tel: 037 881 3532

Polishing and Finishing Supplies (Chap. 4):

Blackfriars: E. Parsons & Sons Ltd, Blackfriars Rd, Nailsea, Bristol BS19 2BU. Tel: 02755 854911.

Colron: Sterling-Roncraft, Chapeltown, Sheffield 530 4YP

Fiddes & Son, Trade St, Cardiff, Tel: 0222 23047

Henry Flack Ltd (all kinds of products, including Briwax and Sheradale) Borough Works, Croydon Rd, Beckenham, Kent BR3 4BI. Tel: 01-650 9171/6

Joy-Plane; Turnbridges Ltd, 72 Longley Rd, London SW 17. Tel: 01-672 6581

Two-part bleach (p. 44) and Plastic Coating (p. 48):

Rustins Ltd, Waterloo Rd, London NW2 7TX. Tel: 01-450 4666

Stencils (p. 83):

Lyn Le Grice, Alsia Mill, St. Buryan, Nr. Penzance, Cornwall. Tel: 0736-72-765

Dip 'n Strip

FRANCHISES:

Brighton, Sussex: Mr Ken Galbraith, tel: 0273 422966
Christchurch, Dorset: Mr Bruce Mew, tel: 0202 476976
Crediton, Devon: Mr Bruce Mew, tel: 03632 5263
Darlington, Co. Durham: Mr Bryan Robson, tel: 0325 480217
Edinburgh, Scotland: Mr Callum Glen, tel: 031 337 0555
Gateshead, Tyne & Wear: Mr & Mrs Ian Harris, tel: 0632 824114
Glasgow, Scotland: Mr Alasdair McPherson, tel: 041 952 9111
Huddersfield, Yorks: Mr & Mrs Michael Howley, tel: 0484 513696
Leeds, Yorks: Mr Len Davies, tel: 0532 445466
Leicester, Mr Alan Hutchby, tel: 0533 769276
Maidstone, Kent: Mr Mick Willey & Mr Jim Lovett, tel: 0622 683308
Norwich, Norfolk: Mrs Lyn Mackenzie, tel: 0603 20529

Plymouth, Devon: Mr Peter Wilderspin, tel: 0752 345900
Portsmouth, Hants: Mr Chris Hoy & Mr Pat Simpson, tel: 0705 698124
Romford, Essex: Mr & Mrs Ralph Corner, tel: 0708 60444
Sheffield, Yorks: Mr & Mrs Istvan Babinski, tel: 0742 755022
St Albans, Herts: Mr Peter Lake, tel: 56 37575

Book list

Affordable Splendour, Diana Phipps, Weidenfeld & Nicolson, London, 1982
Care and Repair of Furniture, Desmond Gaston, Collins, London, 1977
The English Country Chair, Ivan Sparkes, Spurbooks, Bourne End, Bucks, 1977
Encyclopaedia of Antique Restoration and Maintenance, Studio Vista, London, 1974
The Furniture Doctor, George Grotz, Barrie and Jenkins, London, 1979
The Furniture Lover's Book, L. Donald Myers, Van Nostrand Reinhold, New York, 1981
Furniture Refinishing, Harry Wicks, Muller, London, 1977
Heal's Catalogues 1853–1934, David & Charles, Newton Abbot, reprint 1972
Paint Magic, Jocasta Innes, Frances Lincoln, London, 1981
The Pauper's Homemaking Book, Jocasta Innes, Penguin, London, 1978
The Woodworker's Pocket Book, C.H. Hayward, Evans, London, 1980

Index